WITHDRAWN

Excellence

Can We Be Equal and Excellent Too?

Excellence

Can We Be Equal and Excellent Too?

JOHN W. GARDNER

LIBRARY
BRYAN COLLEGE
DAYTON, TN. 37321

PERENNIAL LIBRARY
Harper & Row, Publishers
New York • Hagerstown
San Francisco • London

56557

EXCELLENCE

Copyright © 1961 by John W. Gardner. All rights reserved.
Printed in the United States of America. No part of this book
may be used or reproduced in any manner without written
permission except in the case of brief quotations embodied
in critical articles and reviews. For information address
Harper & Row, Publishers, Inc., 10 East 53rd Street, New
York, N.Y. 10022.

First PERENNIAL LIBRARY edition published 1971.

STANDARD BOOK NUMBER: 06–080223–5

6–77

TO MY MOTHER AND BROTHER

Contents

Acknowledgments

Jean Grolier, the great French book collector, placed inscriptions on the bindings of some of his books which indicated that the volumes belonged to "Io. Grolieri et amicorum" (J. Grolier and his friends). This book should bear a comparable inscription—not on the binding but on the title page. Most authors incur obligations, but I feel that my debt is heavier than most.

First of all I must thank my generous and steadfast colleagues in Carnegie Corporation. Some of them read and commented on the first draft of the book; all of them put up with the heavy drain on my time and energies which authorship entails. I am particularly grateful to James A. Perkins, Florence Anderson, Frederick H. Jackson, Margaret E. Mahoney, Helen Rowan, John C. Honey, Lloyd N. Morrisett and Rosalinde B. Kaufman. Isabelle C. Neilson, whose devotion to excellence has been lifelong, assisted me at every stage of the book. The intelligent help of Helen C. Allen and the extremely competent assistance of Lonnie A. Sharpe were also deeply appreciated.

I owe a special debt of gratitude to those friends who took time from their busy schedules to read the manuscript and to give me the discerning guidance every author needs: Thomas R. Carskadon, Paul R. Farnsworth, Charles Frankel, Harold N. Graves, Caryl P. Haskins, Mrs. Marquis James, John M. Stalnaker, John D. Wilson and Dael Wolfle.

A special note of thanks is due to Lawrence A. Cremin and Julian P. Boyd, who supplied me with interesting and useful source material on certain of the subjects in the book.

Finally, the debt one never manages to acknowledge fully—the debt to one's family. My wife helped with suggestions at every stage. Both of my daughters, Stephanie and Francesca, read and commented on the manuscript, much to the benefit of the final version.

But deep as is my debt to friends and family, I cannot burden them with responsibility for what is in the book. In this an author can only emulate Sir Thomas More on the occasion of his execution. Approaching the steps of the scaffold, he asked the lieutenant to give him a hand going up, but quickly added, "Coming down, I will shift for myself."

JOHN W. GARDNER

Introduction

In the 1930's, Senator Huey Long, "The King-fish," set new standards of demagoguery in this country with his slogans "Every Man a King" and "Share the Wealth." The phrases were politically potent for Long's constituency, but also widely parroted in a humorous way. So it did not surprise me when, as a young professor, I encountered them one day in altered form on the blackboard of my classroom. It was the day of the final exam, and someone had scrawled on the board "Every Man an A-Student!" and below it "Share the Grades!"

It was all in fun, and the culprit turned out to be one of my best students. But the phrases ground themselves into my mind. Lurking behind the words were some interesting social meanings. It was not hard to detect in the educational world of the 1930's echoes of the same equalitarianism that rang in those phrases.

The subject has never ceased to interest me. This is a book about excellence, more particularly about the conditions under which excellence is possible in our kind of society; but it is also—inevitably—a book about equality, about the kinds of equality that can and must be honored, and the kinds that cannot be forced.

Such a book must raise some questions which Americans have shown little inclination to discuss rationally.

What are the characteristic difficulties a democracy encounters in pursuing excellence? Is there a way out of these difficulties?

How equal do we want to be? How equal *can* we be?

What do we mean when we say, "Let the best man win"? Can an equalitarian society tolerate winners?

Are we overproducing highly educated people? How much talent can the society absorb? Does society owe a living to talent? Does talent invariably have a chance to exhibit itself in our society?

Does every young American have a "right" to a college education?

Are we headed toward domination by an intellectual elite?

Is it possible for a people to achieve excellence if they don't believe in anything? Have the American people lost their sense of purpose and the drive which would make it possible for them to achieve excellence?

I have discussed these matters with a great variety of individuals and groups throughout the country, and I find that "excellence" is a curiously powerful word—a word about which people feel strongly and deeply. But it is a word that means different things to different people. It is a little like those ink blots that psychologists use to interpret personality. As the individual contemplates the word "excellence" he reads into it his own aspirations, his own conception of high standards, his hopes for a better world. And it brings powerfully to his mind evidence of the betrayal of excellence (as he conceives it). He thinks not only of the greatness we might achieve but of the mediocrity we have fallen into.

These highly individual reactions to the word excellence create difficulties for the writer or speaker concerned with the subject. When one has had his say, someone is certain to mutter, "How could he talk about excellence without mentioning the Greeks?" And another, "He didn't say a word about the plight of the artist" . . . "Nor teachers' salaries" . . . "Nor the organization man!"

It isn't just that people have different opinions about excellence. They see it from different vantage points. The elementary school teacher preoccupied with instilling respect for standards in seven-year-olds will think about it in one way. The literary critic concerned with understanding and interpreting the highest reaches of creative expression will think of it in a wholly different way. The statesman, the composer, the intellectual historian—each will raise his own questions and pose the issues which are important for him.

It will help the reader to know what my own

vantage point is. I am concerned with the social context in which excellence may survive or be smothered. I am concerned with the fate of excellence in our kind of society. This preoccupation may lead me to neglect some of the interesting and perplexing problems of excellence as these confront the specialist striving for the highest reaches of performance in his particular field. I am sorry that such neglect must occur, but I leave its repair to other writers. This book is concerned with the difficult, puzzling, delicate and important business of toning up a whole society, of bringing a whole people to that fine edge of morale and conviction and zest that makes for greatness.

This is not a Utopian tract. Some of those who complain about the quality of our national life seem to be dreaming of a world in which everyone without exception has talent, taste, judgment and an unswerving allegiance to excellence. Such dreams are pleasant but unprofitable. The problem is to achieve some measure of excellence *in this society*, with all its beloved and exasperating clutter, with all its exciting and debilitating confusion of standards, with all the stubborn problems that won't be solved and the equally stubborn ones that might be.

Some aspects of excellence have been the subject of extensive and authoritative treatment. The whole field of literary criticism, for example, may be regarded as one long exercise in appraising, understanding, defining and savoring excellence in one important area of human activity. But the subject with which I shall deal has received relatively little attention. And this is not surprising, because it involves complex and controversial social issues, some of which Americans find it downright embarrassing to talk about.

This book deals with only one of the many problems facing a free society. But it is a problem that cuts across all the others. If a society holds conflicting views about excellence—or cannot rouse itself to the pursuit of excellence—the consequences will be felt in everything that it undertakes. The disease may not attack every organ, but the resulting debility will be felt in all parts of the system. Everything that it does and everything that it strives for will be affected.

part one

Equal and Unequal

chapter I

The Decline of Hereditary Privilege

You Can *Keep a Good Man Down*

If we accept the common usage of words, nothing can be more readily disproved than the old saw, "You can't keep a good man down." Most human societies have been beautifully organized to keep good men down. Of course there are irrepressible spirits who burst all barriers; but on the whole, human societies have severely and successfully limited the realization of individual promise. They did not set out consciously to achieve that goal. It is just that full realization of individual promise is not possible on a wide scale in societies of hereditary privilege—and most human societies have had precisely that characteristic. They have been systems in which the individual's status was determined not by his gifts or capacities but by his membership in a family, a caste or a class. Such membership determined his rights, privileges, prestige, power and status in the society. His ability was hardly relevant.

The faithful family servant of a thousand Victorian novels described one aspect of such a society by saying, "I know my place." And Molly Malone—who was part of such an order—sang, "My father and mother were fishmongers too." Birth determined occupation and status. It determined whom you bowed to, who bowed to you, the weight of your voice in the community and the kinds of suitors who sought your daughter's hand.

Such societies were doomed by the Industrial Revolution. It was essential to the new modes of economic organization that the individual be free to bargain (and be bargained for) in the open market on the basis of his capacity to perform, without regard to other criteria of status. But the Industrial Revolution was not the only factor in bringing a new measure of autonomy to the individual. The seventeenth and eighteenth centuries had seen the emergence of religious ideas which laid great stress on individual responsibility. Tawney remarked of the Puritan that he was a natural republican, "for there is none on earth that he can own as master." [1] * And eighteenth-century ideas of democracy demanded that the individual be allowed to function politically regardless of hereditary status. Thomas Jefferson, borrowing a vivid phrase from an English revolutionary, said, ". . . the mass of mankind has not been born with saddles on their backs, nor a favored few booted and

* Superior numbers refer to a section of notes beginning on page 197.

spurred, ready to ride them legitimately, by the grace of God." [2]

But although religious and political forces were powerful allies in loosening the web of hereditary privilege, it was the Industrial Revolution that forced the issue. Once its full impact was felt, societies of hereditary status could never again be quite the same. The only question was what would come next. We shall concern ourselves here with only one aspect of what came next, namely, the ways in which the new societies dealt with differences in individual ability and performance.

It is one of the ironies of history that reformers so often misjudge the consequences of their reforms. Most of those who fought to abolish social hierarchies saw the stratified society as a device for maintaining artificial differences between men, and they imagined that the removal of that artificiality would greatly diminish such differences. It was clear to Rousseau and his followers, for example, that it was simply a matter of dissolving the false relationships into which society had forced men and restoring them to their natural state. But the truth is that when men are released from the fetters on performance characteristic of a stratified society, great individual differences in performance will emerge, and may lead to peaks and valleys of status as dramatic as those produced by hereditary stratification. Many a feudal lord would have given his drawbridge to enjoy the power and glory of the industrial barons who pushed him into the history books.

When a society gives up hereditary stratification, there are two ways in which it may deal with the dramatic individual differences in ability and performance that emerge. One way is to limit or work against such individual differences, protecting the slow runners and curbing the swift. This is the path of equalitarianism. The other way is simply to "let the best man win." As we shall see, in their moderate forms each of these points of view—equalitarianism and competitive performance—is a necessary ingredient of a healthy society (as we conceive health in a society). We shall also note that each point of view can be carried to harmful extremes.

Each position, in its more moderate form, represents a facet of the American ideal. "Zwei Seelen wohnen, ach! in meiner Brust," Faust said. The "two souls" in the breast of every American are the devotion to equalitarianism and the attachment to individual achievement. If you say to the average American that all men should be equal, he will say, "Of course!" And if you then say that we should "let the best man win," he will applaud this as a noble thought. The idea that the two views might often conflict doesn't occur to him. His sentiments are those of the Irishman who cried, "I'm as good as you are, and a great deal better too!"

In their extreme forms the two positions are mutually exclusive. But very few societies have encouraged anything approaching extreme equalitarianism (certainly the Soviet Union has not); and very few have come close to an unbridled emphasis upon competitive performance.

It is easy for us as Americans to see positive virtue in both equalitarianism *and* emphasis upon competitive performance. But it is not easy for us to see the disadvantages of either. The drama which still grips our national imagination is the escape from a society of hereditary privilege. And our aversion to such a society is so great as to cast any alternatives in a positive light. As a result, any bright schoolboy can write an essay on the disadvantages of hereditary stratification. Hardly any could write an essay on the disadvantages of extreme equalitarianism or of extreme emphasis upon individual performance. But such essays must be written.

The Stubborn Vitality of Nephewism

First, however, we must look more closely at the principle of hereditary privilege. Because Americans dislike the principle, we tend not to talk about it. To the extent that it characterizes our social arrangements, we try to ignore it.

But ignoring it does not make it go away. Only the nations most profoundly affected by the Industrial Revolution discarded the strict patterns of hereditary stratification. The majority of societies in the world, even today, have not truly assimilated the Industrial Revolution, and thus have not experienced those volcanic forces which shattered traditional patterns in the more modern countries. Most so-called "underdeveloped" societies show a high degree of stratification. In Africa today one may observe hereditary tribal leadership existing alongside newer forms of representative government in the same community. It is correct to say that the consequences are confusing.

But even in those countries which received the full impact of the Industrial Revolution, the old way of organizing society held on with surprising stubbornness. Anyone familiar with contemporary Western Europe knows that the older forms show remarkable strength even today.

Hereditary privilege has been relatively weak in the United States, which acquired its distinctive character at precisely the time in history when the old ways were under most vigorous attack and the new ways gaining their first foothold. The colonists left the old patterns behind them, and found in America a *tabula rasa* on which to sketch the character of a new society. Much the same may be said of Australia, New Zealand and Canada, which also developed after the old forms of social organization had lost their grip.

Yet even in the United States one finds unmistakable vestiges of a stratified society. The "old families" of Boston, Philadelphia, Baltimore and Charleston may have grown a bit moldy, but they have survived. Vestiges of an earlier way of thinking about social class may be observed in the society columns of the newspapers, in the fashionable prep schools, in the exclusive clubs, and even in the casual conversation of many Americans.

The truth is that the characteristics of human interaction and social organization that produced societies of hereditary privilege in the first place have not changed. Indeed, the tendency toward hereditary stratification is so deeply rooted in human interaction that if one could miraculously eliminate every trace of it today, it would begin to creep back tomorrow. Every father is a potential dynast. (Ask any college admissions officer.)

This is not to say that the newer forms of social organization are ephemeral, nor that we should anticipate the return of aristocracies in the old pattern. It does mean that the older forms of social organization grew out of something enduring in the process of human interaction and that, given appropriate circumstances, this "something enduring" could easily re-create patterns we thought we had put behind us.

The newer principles—equalitarianism on the one hand and competitive performance on the other—are not easy to live with in the day-to-day round of existence. There are many individuals who can never be entirely happy in a world which judges each man on the basis of what he can do, or deals with all in a framework of unrelieved equality. Literally no one is likely to find unqualified pleasure in such arrangements.

There are many times in the life of each individual when he is delighted to accept some good thing which comes to him not because he earned it, and not because it was his equal share of something everyone else got too, but simply because he stood in a family relationship to the donor, or occupied a certain position in the community, or was a member of the same club as the donor. Similarly, almost every man who makes decisions with respect to others—recruitment, promotions, job assignments and the like —has occasionally based those decisions not strictly on performance or character or an equal sharing of favors, but on the fact that the man involved was a relative, a friend or a parishioner of the same church. This is a far cry from a society of hereditary status. But it is the seed from which such societies grow. Any favoritism which judges the individual on the basis of his relationships rather than on ability and character is a seed which, properly nourished, can eventually produce a full-blown society of hereditary status.

This is true of nepotism—literally *nephewism* —wherever it occurs: in business, in government or in any other organization. When the grand old man who founded a corporation forty years ago moves up to the board chairmanship and places his son in the president's office, he is doing his bit to move society back toward a system of hereditary status. The mayor of a Western city was recently under political attack for having placed no less than fourteen relatives in city jobs. The fraternity which gives special consideration to "legacies" (i.e., relatives of present members), the college which gives special consideration to sons of alumni, the clubs which weigh family background in selecting new members, the mother who doesn't want her son to marry "below his station"—all are examples of the continuing vigor of the forces leading back toward hereditary stratification.

The most spectacular examples of stratified societies that we know anything about are ones in which social class lines have formed and crystallized over centuries. As a result we tend to think of such stratification as a slow growth. In its fully elaborated form, no doubt it is; but its more rudimentary forms may emerge very rapidly. There is probably no town in this country so young that it does not have its local aristocracy.

But no local aristocracy—old or new—has much of a future. And since aristocracies based on "social position," in the society-page sense of that phrase, are always primarily local, this suggests that their days are numbered. In our transient society, with its constant movement of population, it is difficult for such aristocracies to maintain their authority and to keep intact the fiction of their superior quality.

Observers who are curious about such matters might be far wiser to keep a sharp eye on *aristocracies of profession*. These have rather impressive survival value in our present social structure. One is bound to note and reflect on the number of academic children of academic parents, military children of military parents, and so forth. Even in the second generation of such families one gains a remarkably strong impression of entrenched attitudes, of a sense of membership in a special world and of a developing separation from the world at large.

At a reception following the commencement ceremony at one of our leading universities, a biologist whom I had known for years introduced me to his prospective son-in-law, and confided later that he was disappointed in his daughter's choice. I asked about his objections to the lad (who had impressed me very well). Was he stupid? No. Lazy? No. Ill-tempered? No. Finally my friend grinned wryly and said, "He works in a bank. He even wants to be president of it eventually."

"Is that bad?" I asked.

"Well, no . . . but I had hoped she'd pick a scientist—or at least an academic man. I don't even know how to talk to a banker!"

chapter II

Equality and Competitive Performance

All Shall Equal Be

During the California gold rush, Mrs. Clappe, a physician's wife living in one of the mining camps on the north fork of the Feather River, made the following entry in her journal:

Sept. 4, 1852

Last night one of our neighbors had a dinner party. He came in to borrow a teaspoon. "Had you not better take them all?" I said. "Oh, no," was the answer, "that would be too much luxury. My guests are not used to it, and they would think that I was getting aristocratic, and putting on airs. One is enough; they can pass it 'round from one to the other." [1]

It was from such frontier conditions that much of our equalitarianism sprang. Americans love the idea of equality. In intellectual terms they may be confused as to what it implies, but emotionally they are not in doubt. They love it.

But what is it that they love? The incident on the Feather River gives no clue to the enduring content of American equalitarianism. Our devotion to the one-spoon dining service has not proved durable. What does equality mean for Americans?

The truth is that Americans in general are more than a little confused on the subject. Still, it is possible to suggest the views concerning equality which would probably receive general endorsement in this country today. First of all, we believe that in the final matters of life and death all men are equally worthy of our care and concern. "We come equals into this world," said George Mason in 1775, "and equals shall we go out of it." [2] Chesterton meant something not very different when he reminded us that in an accident at sea we do not cry, "Bad citizen overboard!" [3]

Beyond this we believe that men are equal in the possession of certain legal, civil and political rights. We believe with Aristotle that "the only stable state is the one in which all men are equal before the law." [4]

But we know that men are not equal in their native gifts nor in their motivations; and it follows that they will not be equal in their achievements. That is why we have given *equality of opportunity* such a central role in our social philosophy. "We may not all hit home runs," the saying goes, "but every man should have his chance at bat."

At the same time one must admit that the idea of equality of opportunity is not as simple as it sounds. In practice it means an equal chance to compete within the framework of goals and the structure of rules established by our particular society; and this tends to favor certain kinds of people with certain kinds of gifts. The society may insure my child equality of opportunity with every other child. But it can only place before him (and before all other children) the range of opportunities available in this particular society. If his undiscovered talent is for chariot racing or if he has the capacity to see visions, he has missed his century. This is unavoidable. But it is only proper to recognize that even if a society achieved perfect equality of opportunity, it would still inevitably favor those whose gifts fit the requirements of that society.

We must recognize that we are far from having achieved equality of opportunity. In a society in which there are great differences in wealth, learning and concern for education, free schooling may never compensate for the tremendous variations in opportunity represented by home background. When a New York social worker asked a Puerto Rican youngster whether there were any books in his home, the boy nodded proudly. "The telephone book," he explained. We cannot rest easy in the face of such inequality of circumstance. It is not enough to assert our devotion to equality of opportunity. We must make it a reality.

So much for the conception of equality which would win almost universal acceptance in the United States today. Some Americans have gone considerably beyond this in their equalitarian views, insisting that no man should be regarded as better than another man in any dimension, and that there should be no differences in status whatever.

Equalitarians holding these extreme views have tended to believe that men of great leadership capacities, great energies or greatly superior aptitudes are more trouble to society than they are worth. Lionel Trilling says ". . . all the instincts or necessities of radical democracy are against the superbness and arbitrariness which often mark great spirits." [5] Merle Curti reminds us that in the Jacksonian era in this country equalitarianism reached such heights that trained personnel in the public service were considered unnecessary. "The democratic faith further held that no special group might mediate between the common man and the truth, even though trained competence might make the difference between life and death." [6] Thus, in the West, even licensing of physicians was lax, because not to be lax was apt to be thought undemocratic!

This same impulse may be observed in some of our local political contests, in which voters favor the candidate whose folksy, ungrammatical, thumb-in-suspenders style seems to say that he is not in any respect superior to the average voter, and is perhaps a little inferior. "Friends, red-necks, suckers, and fellow hicks" was Willie Stark's greeting to the voters.[7]

The same attitudes are observable in the widespread social pressure to play down one's gifts. One of the requirements of social effectiveness in many segments of our national life is that one not arouse envy through an unseemly display of intelligence or talent. One must be, above all, unthreatening to the other fellow's self-esteem. In this atmosphere it will surprise no one to learn that deliberately slovenly speech, the studied fumble and the calculated inelegance have achieved the status of minor art forms. And the phrase "I'm just a country boy" has become the favored gambit of sophisticated and wily men.

We have seen enough of extreme equalitarianism to know what it involves. We have seen mediocrity breed mediocrity. We now understand what Kierkegaard meant when he warned us of the danger of an equalitarianism so extreme as to be "unrelieved by even the smallest eminence." [8]

We might as well admit that it is not easy for us as believers in democracy to dwell on the differences in capacity between men. Democratic philosophy has tended to ignore such differences where possible, and to belittle them where it could not ignore them. And it has had some grounds for doing so: the enemies of democracy have often cited the unequal capacities of men as an excuse for institutions which violate our most deeply held beliefs. But extreme equalitarianism—or as I would prefer to say, *equalitarianism wrongly conceived*—which ignores differences in native capacity and achievement, has not served democracy well. Carried far enough, it means the lopping off of any heads which come above dead level. It means committee rule, the individual smothered by the group. And it means the end of that striving for excellence which has produced mankind's greatest achievements.

Although the United States has never chosen the path of extreme equalitarianism, the philosophy has many—perhaps unwitting—adherents in our midst. And this will not change.

To sum up, then: In its moderate forms, equalitarianism prohibits ruthlessness in the strong, protects the weak from wanton injury and defines certain areas of equality which must not be transgressed, but does not seek altogether to eliminate individual differences or their consequences. Moderate equalitarianism has produced innumerable measures which most enlightened Americans regard as essential: minimum-wage laws, the graduated income tax and the principle that each citizen has one vote—to mention only a few. In its extreme forms, equalitarianism denies that there are inequalities in capacity, eliminates the situations in which such inequalities can exhibit themselves and insures that if such differences do emerge, they will not result in differences in status.

Let the Best Man Win

The counterpoise to equalitarianism in the American ethos has been our keen interest in individual performance. Many Americans have always assumed that the only sensible way to organize society is to allow each individual to enjoy whatever status, privileges and power he is capable of winning for himself out of the general striving. Americans have a genuine fondness for this conception, and most would assert that it describes fairly well our whole approach to social organization.

In its more moderate forms, the emphasis upon individual achievement has been highly salutary. No feature of our own society is more highly treasured today than the opportunity for every man to realize the promise that is in him, and to achieve status in terms of his own performance. Frederick Jackson Turner wrote:

Western democracy through the whole of its earlier period tended to the production of a society of which the most distinctive fact was the freedom of the individual to rise under conditions of social mobility . . .[9]

These are values we would never willingly relinquish. Abraham Lincoln, born in a log cabin; Andrew Carnegie, the son of a poor Scottish weaver; Ezra Cornell, starting life as a carpenter and mill hand—these are favored snapshots in our national family album. In 1856, when a statue of Benjamin Franklin was unveiled in Boston, the principal speaker said:

"Behold him, ye that are humblest and poorest in present condition or in future prospect,—lift up your heads and look at the image of a man who rose from

nothing, who owed nothing to parentage or patronage
. . . but who lived to stand before kings, . . ." [10]

Woodrow Wilson wisely observed that democracy "releases the energies of every human
being," and this was one of the most significant
consequences of the dissolution of stratified
societies. The United States, which has perhaps
moved further in emphasizing individual performance than any other nation, has been known
from its earliest days for the sheer vigor and
activity of its citizens. Some contemporary observers talk as though our extraordinarily high
level of activity were a product of the mid-
twentieth century, a neurotic symptom of our
late middle age, born of our anxieties and nourished by hucksters. Nothing can be further from
the truth.

"No sooner do you set foot upon American
ground," said de Tocqueville in 1835, "than
you are stunned by a kind of tumult. Everything
is in motion . . ." [11] Said another observer, "A
feverish activity seems to obsess these inhabit-
ants of North America." [12] And Alistair Cooke
said in 1952, "America may end in spontaneous
combustion, but never in apathy, inertia or un-
inventiveness." [13]

Societies of hereditary privilege kept a lid on
the aspirations of most individuals. With the
lid removed, aspirations soared. Men dared to
hope, and they dared act in pursuit of their
hopes. And constantly reinforcing their hope

was the drama of "hidden gifts discovered." Few themes have gripped the imagination of Americans so intensely as the discovery of talent in unexpected places—the slum child who shows scientific genius, the frail youngster who develops athletic skills, the poor boy who becomes a captain of industry. Our popular literature and our folklore are full of such images. They encourage self-discovery, stir ambition and inspire emulation. The American who wins success overnight traditionally insists, "I never dreamed it could happen to me!" But as surely as he is an American, that is precisely what he did dream.

The vividness of these dreams is convincing evidence that emphasis on competitive performance is still an American habit. A more objective line of evidence is the impressive increase in the use of standardized aptitude and achievement tests. Neither a society of hereditary privilege nor a profoundly equalitarian society would use such tests with enthusiasm.

But release from hereditary stratification brought problems as well as opportunities for the individual. Sometimes it gave him only the freedom to be crushed by the new forces of industrial society. And while it offered him freedom to achieve, it placed a new burden of responsibility and pressure on him. Among the consequences were not only exhilaration but anxiety, not only self-discovery but fear. The stratified society had its own grim pressures, and produced frustration in many gifted and highly motivated people, but it was a source of security for many others.

Like equalitarianism, emphasis on individual performance can be pushed to extremes; and we now know that there are hazards in such extremes. "Everyone for himself and the Devil take the hindmost" is a colorful saying but an unworkable model for social organization. No society has ever fully tested this manner of organizing human relationships—for the very good reason that any society which carried the principle to its logical conclusion would tear itself to pieces. The laws against mayhem and murder, for example, are designed to prevent ruthless members of society from enjoying the fruits of their ruthlessness.

But even within the bounds of the law, extreme emphasis on performance as a criterion of status may foster an atmosphere of raw striving that results in brutal treatment of the less able, or less vigorous, or less aggressive; it may wantonly injure those whose temperament or whose values make them unwilling to engage in performance rivalries; it may penalize those whose undeniable excellences do not add up to the kinds of performance that society at any given moment chooses to reward.

Some of the casualties of such a system were paraded before the Ashley Mines Investigation Commission in England in 1842, among them Sarah Gooder. Here is Sarah's view of a world she never made:

"I am Sarah Gooder, I am eight years old. I'm a coal carrier in the Gawber Mine. It does not tire me, but I have to trap without a light and I'm scared. I go at four and sometimes half past three in the morning, and come out at five and half past in the evening. I never go to sleep. Sometimes I sing when I've light, but not in the dark; I dare not sing then. I don't like being in the pit. I am very sleepy when I go in in the morning. I go to Sunday school and learn to read. They teach me to pray. I have heard tell of Jesus many a time. I don't know why he came on earth. I don't know why he died, but he had stones for his head to rest on." [14]

But the brutalities of the early days of the Industrial Revolution were not the only sources of difficulty. There were other and more subtle hazards yet to come.

In a society of hereditary privilege, an individual of humble position might not have been wholly happy with his lot, but he had never had reason to look forward to any other fate. Never having had prospects of betterment, he could hardly be disillusioned. He entertained no hopes, but neither was he nagged by ambition. When the new democracies removed the ceiling on expectations, nothing could have been more satisfying for those with the energy, ability and emotional balance to meet the challenge. But to the individual lacking in these qualities, the new system was fraught wth danger. Lack of ability, lack of energy or lack of aggressiveness led to frustration and failure. Obsessive ambition led to emotional breakdown. Unrealistic ambitions led to bitter defeats.

No system which issues an open invitation to every youngster to "shoot high" can avoid facing the fact that room at the top is limited. Donald Paterson reports that *four-fifths* of our young people aspire to high-level jobs, of which there are only enough to occupy *one-fifth* of our labor force.[15] Such figures conceal a tremendous amount of human disappointment.

To sum up: In its moderate forms, emphasis on individual achievement allows a healthy play to individual gifts, holds out an invitation to excel but does not necessarily sanction the ruthless subordination of those who are less able, less vigorous or less aggressive. Thus in our own society the able youngster can rise from humble beginnings—but he is limited in the way he can use his superior ability as a means of exploiting or subordinating others. In its extreme forms, the let-the-best-man-win philosophy can lead to something close to the law of the jungle: let those who can, survive; let others go under. The first half-century of the Industrial Revolution produced abundant examples of this philosophy in its more extreme form. With the weakening of the principle of hereditary status, not only the most able but the most aggressive and ruthless moved to positions of power, and those less able to compete suffered bitterly.

The United States has never committed itself to extreme emphasis upon individual performance, but at times it has come close.

chapter III

The Three-Way Contest

Note that the three competing principles—hereditary privilege, equalitarianism and competitive performance—may all be present in the same society. They are certainly present in our own. The relative strength of the three principles may vary from one activity to another within the same society. For example, there are American communities which are fairly stratified in the strictly social dimension of life, relatively equalitarian in education and inclined to let the best man win in economic matters.

And to complicate the picture further, the three principles do not always function independently. The adherents of any two of them may form an alliance to attack the third, and this produces curious anomalies in social interaction. The aristocrat and the thoroughgoing equalitarian can find common ground in their dislike of the successful self-made man, and will sometimes combine against him. For his part, he returns the hostility, knowing that he could not have risen so easily either in a purely aristocratic society or in a fully equalitarian one.

At other times, the self-made men in a society may readily form an alliance with the aristocratic elements in order to combat equalitarian movements. Indeed this alliance—of old families and new dollars—has been the foundation stone of American political conservatism.

Men of great ability and ambition are not apt to be strong proponents of equalitarianism. But here again we find alliances of convenience. The discovery by vigorous leaders that alliance with the masses could carry them to their objectives is as old as recorded history.

When David was in the cave of Adullam, "everyone that was in distress, and everyone that was in debt, and everyone that was discontented, gathered themselves unto him; and he became a captain over them. . . ." [1]

In G.B. Shaw's *The Apple Cart*, the demagogue Boanerges describes his technique for dealing with the people:

"I talk democracy to these men and women. I tell them that they have the vote, and that theirs is the kingdom and the power and the glory. I say to them, 'You are supreme: exercise your power.' They say, 'That's right: tell us what to do'; and I tell them. I say, 'Exercise your vote intelligently by voting for me.' And they do. That's democracy; and a splendid thing it is too for putting the right men in the right place." [2]

With the recent increase in mass movements it has become downright conventional for power-hungry men to ally themselves with the masses as a means of achieving political glory. Elaborate procedures have been developed to insure the success of the maneuver, and highly skilled practitioners have emerged. Huey Long was a brilliant performer in the new phase of the ancient art. Juan Perón was another.

Perhaps the most significant thing that can be said about the contest among the three principles as it goes on today is that when any one of them moves into something approaching a dominating position, it creates conditions which work toward its own downfall. To put it another way, each principle in its extreme application is highly unstable and vulnerable. In the long centuries when the society of hereditary privilege held the stage without worthy opponents, it could become exceedingly vulnerable without being overthrown. But now that both equalitarianism and the idea of individual achievement have reached fairly mature development, this could not occur.

The root weaknesses of hereditary stratification in its most fully developed form are lowered vitality, dry rot and the strangling of individual initiative by the tyranny of hereditary roles. Any stratified society may have a brilliant period of flowering. But all too often the ablest and most dynamic men in the society, curbed by gradations of rank and the fetters of social custom, are unable to realize their creative potentialities. Everything settles into the deep grooves of prescribed social procedure. Such conditions today would open a stratified society to devastating onslaught at the hands of those dynamic groups who hold opposing philosophies.

The extremes of equalitarianism are also unstable and vulnerable. People have innumerable reasons for wanting, needing and enjoying vigorous leadership. And gifted, hard-driving people are usually available to supply that need. When an organization under the suppressing force of extreme equalitarianism reaches a sufficiently dead level of mediocrity, it may be ready prey to the vitality of men who are prepared to step in with personal force and initiative.

Indeed under conditions of equalitarianism gifted individuals may even develop intensified drives for excellence. Harold Nicolson has suggested that what he regards as a depressing atmosphere of mediocrity in England today may be more stimulating to the occasional genius than would the presence of innumerable competing geniuses! [3] In this connection, it has always struck me as a matter of singular interest that Edmund Hillary came out of the flattest social landscape in the world and climbed the highest mountain in the world. Geographically New Zealand is all peaks and valleys, but socially it is a featureless plain. What that may have contributed to Sir Edmund's great performance is a matter for speculation.

Finally, extreme emphasis on competitive performance also makes a society vulnerable. In an organization or society which places exclusive emphasis on individual performance there arise such searing rivalries, such intense competition, such a pervading insecurity that the organization may be virtually pulled apart at the seams. Large numbers of individuals within the organization develop a fierce desire to find shelter from the chill wind of unmitigated competition. Powerful internal forces soon combine to alter a state of affairs which is tolerable to very few in the organization or society.

It is sometimes said that while the ordinary mortal dreads excessive competition, the businessman loves it. But the record shows that businessmen can move very swiftly to protect themselves against the harsher manifestations of competition. Out of this impulse come price-fixing agreements and innumerable other highly effective devices in restraint of trade.

Extreme emphasis on competitive performance in an organization (or society) leads to one kind of vulnerability. Extreme equalitarianism leads to another kind. The former produces consequences which are threatening to so many people within an organization (or society) that there arise powerful *internal* forces to combat the emphasis. On the other hand, in an organization or society characterized by extreme equalitarianism the greatest threat lies in *external competition,* i.e., from aggressive organizations or societies which have *not* fettered their most talented and energetic people.

This holds an important lesson for us as a nation. To the extent that we move toward dangerous excesses of emphasis on competitive performance, we can probably count on self-corrective forces from within our own society. To the extent that we move toward excesses of equalitarianism, we may learn our lesson only at the hands of more vigorous outsiders.

There has been much discussion of the role of the large organization in modern society. It will be useful to consider briefly the way in which the three contesting philosophies relate to modern organization.

First of all, it should be obvious that the modern large organization could not have emerged without the disappearance of hereditary stratification in its strict form. There have been large organizations throughout history. But in their modern form they require, among other things, flexible movement and interchange of people *on the basis of their usefulness to the organization*. This is impossible in a society which determines status on the basis of relationship. You can't give the Prince of Wales an aptitude test and start him in the stock room.

But though the modern organization could come into being only after the passing of the full-blown stratified society, the active ingredient of stratification lingers on in the forms of nepotism and favoritism. So clear and powerful is this tendency that many large organizations have adopted rules designed specifically to prevent it.

One might suppose that the principle most antithetical to the large modern organization would be equalitarianism, since any complex organization is inevitably hierarchical. But the truth is that a rather high degree of equalitarianism is tolerated—even encouraged within many large organizations. It is not an equalitarianism that extends over the organization as a whole, but covers a given level in the hierarchy, reducing the competition which might have characterized relationships at that level. The large organization may strive for efficiency but its members—even its executives—do not necessarily love efficiency. They do love stability. And some of the measures favored by equalitarianism are such as to enhance stability very considerably—by eliminating competition and the unpredictable rearrangements of the power structure produced by able and aggressive people. Thus, particularly in the middle and lower levels of large organizations, there may develop provisions for the strictly equal treatment of individuals within large job categories.

So the large organization is far from inhospitable to some measure of equalitarianism. But it cannot live with the extremes of equalitarianism because it *must* have at its disposal a wide range of human abilities, it must know the nature and degree of these abilities and it must be in a position to reassign people on the basis of these abilities. On this score the large organization resists equalitarianism for precisely the same reason that it resists hereditary stratification. Both make it impossible to deal with individuals strictly on the basis of performance.

Just as the organization would have difficulty in dealing with the son of the founder strictly on merit, so it may have difficulty in dealing with a union member on merit.

The amount of emphasis placed on competitive performance varies greatly from one large organization to another. In some organizations, the incentive system is arranged in such a way as to bring competition among individuals to a fairly lively pitch. In other organizations, a firmly observed hierarchy plus equalitarian relations for those at any given level of the hierarchy combine to limit effective performance. This is the kind of organization in which seniority weighs heavily in promotion, and the chief way to win points is to grow older.

American attitudes toward the three contesting philosophies divide them into two categories. The principle of *hereditary stratification* is the old, bad category. The principles of *equalitarianism* and *competitive performance* fall into the new and good category. (The fact that equalitarianism and competitive performance are often in conflict doesn't diminish our fondness for both.)

It will shed interesting light on the three contesting principles if we look at them from a quite different perspective. Let us think in terms of

1. Emphasis on Individual Performance
2. Restraints on Individual Performance

(a) Hereditary Stratification

(b) Equalitarianism

It may seem odd to lump the principles of stratification and equalitarianism in the same category. Stratification is the principle of aristocratic societies, and equalitarianism is anti-aristocratic. But they have in common the fact that they both impose restraints on individual performance. Both try to keep a lid on individual aspirations. Indeed, extreme equalitarianism might be thought of as an attempt to put back onto aspirations the strait jacket that was ripped off when we put stratified societies behind us.

Both hereditary privilege and extreme equalitarianism protect the individual from judgments made on the basis of performance. The town's leading family tries to protect its duller offspring by resorting to nepotism—which is the seed of hereditary stratification. The union protects its less able members by demanding across-the-board raises and by opposing piece rates. The goals sought by the leading family and the union are identical: to protect the individual against judgments based on performance.

Another way of describing what the two principles have in common is to say that equalitarianism leads to a stratified society with only one stratum.

There is evidence, in short, that the critical lines of tension in our society are between *emphasis on individual performance* and *restraints on individual performance*. This tension will never be resolved and *never should be resolved*. Failure to accept this reality has led to a lot of nervous indigestion and unnecessary commotion.

In the light of these considerations, one may see how archaic are those analyses which treat such matters in terms of labels such as "Jacksonianism" and "Jeffersonianism," or which assume that any position taken with respect to individual differences may be characterized as either "pro-elite" or "pro-masses," as "aristocratic" or "democratic." Such primitive categories serve only to mask reality.

We shall have to be exceedingly clear about these matters if we are to develop a more mature view of democracy itself. No democracy can function effectively until it has gone a long way toward dissolving systems of hereditary stratification. This is presumably true of any democracy, but overwhelmingly true of the urbanized, industrial democracy with which we are familiar. On the other hand, no democracy can give itself over to extreme emphasis on individual performance and still remain a democracy—or to extreme equalitarianism and still retain its vitality.

If democracy is to hold these contesting philosophies in balance, the citizens of democracy must understand the implications of each. We have never been willing to explore those implications candidly and incisively.

part two

Talent

chapter IV

The Great Talent Hunt

The Demand for High-Talent Manpower
Speaking on the campus of Stanford University in 1906, William James said, "The world . . . is only beginning to see that the wealth of a nation consists more than in anything else in the number of superior men that it harbors." [1]

James was generous in suggesting that the world shared his own prophetic understanding. Actually, he was half a century ahead of his time. We are just now coming to grasp the profound truth of his remark.

The fact is that we are witnessing a revolution in society's attitude toward men and women of high ability and advanced training. For the first time in history, such men and women are very much in demand on a very wide scale. Throughout the ages, human societies have always been extravagantly wasteful of talent. Today, as a result of far-reaching social and technological developments in our society, we are forced to search for talent and to use it effectively. Among the historic changes which have marked our era, this may in the long run prove to be one of the most profound.

In recent years the need for men of high ability

and advanced training has often been so pressing in one field or another as to claim national attention. Such attention has frequently ignored broader educational and social goals in favor of "crash" programs to meet the crisis of the moment. When the shortage of engineers first became acute, some people behaved as though no other educational goal could be as important as turning out more engineers. After the Russians put the first satellite into orbit, some of our leaders seemed to be saying that the only conceivable purpose of American education was to pour human material into defense activities. And the human material came to be talked of in much the same terms we use in speaking of our oil or uranium reserves.

All of this has annoyed a good many thoughtful people. And it has led some to suppose that the whole recent emphasis on talent is the work of men whose concern for the Cold War has unhinged their judgment. This view calls for correction. The demand for highly trained talent is, of course, affected by international crises. But its roots lie deeper, and its consequences reach out into every phase of our national life. The demand for talent is an inevitable consequence of our stage of development as a society. As such, it has been rising for a long time. It is not a recent trend. We can observe societies in the world today at every stage of development from the most primitive to the most advanced, and nothing is easier to demonstrate than that every step toward the latter involves a heavier demand for educated talent. As Alfred North Whitehead put it, "In the conditions of modern life the rule is absolute, the race which does not value trained intelligence is doomed." [2]

The demand for high-talent manpower is firmly rooted in the level of technological complexity which characterizes modern life, and in the complexity of modern social organization. And more important than either of these is the *rate of innovation and change* in both technological and social spheres. In a world that is rocking with change we need more than anything else a high capacity for adjustment to changed circumstances, a capacity for innovation. The solutions we hit on today will be outmoded tomorrow. Only high ability and sound education equip a man for the continuous seeking of new solutions. We don't even know what skills may be needed in the years ahead. That is why we must train our ablest young men and women in the fundamental fields of knowledge, and equip them to understand and cope with change. That is why we must give them the critical qualities of mind and the durable qualities of character which will serve them in circumstances we cannot now even predict.

It is not just technical competence which is needed. A society such as ours is dependent upon many kinds of achievement, many kinds of complex understanding. It requires large numbers of individuals with depth of judgment, perspective and a broad comprehension of the problems facing our world.

And the importance of education in modern society is not limited to the higher orders of talent. A complex society is dependent every hour of every day upon the capacity of its people to read and write, to make complex judgments and to act in the light of fairly extensive information. When there is not this kind of base on which to build, modern social and economic developments are simply impossible. And if that base were to disappear suddenly in any complex society, the whole intricate interlocking mechanism would grind to a halt.

The chief means of carrying on the talent hunt is the educational system. Schools not only educate youngsters—they sort them out. When the need for talent is great—as it is today—this sifting tends to become fairly rigorous.

There was a time—a fairly recent time—when education was *not* a rigorous sorting-out process. The demand for individuals of high ability is now so familiar to us as to seem wholly unremarkable, but it constitutes a profound change in human affairs. Throughout the millennia of history, it has been the normal experience of mankind that only a few of the gifted individuals in a population have had the chance to develop their gifts. Generally speaking, individuals whose gifts have been discovered and cultivated have been as chance outcroppings of precious rock, while the great reserves of human talent lay undiscovered below.

In 1900 only about 4 per cent of the college-age population went to college. For every youngster who went on with his schooling, there were many just as bright who did not. The boy without an education could look around and see plenty of able and ambitious young fellows in the same condition. Large numbers of children grew up in areas where schools were poor or nonexistent. Many energetic boys broke off schooling to pull their weight on the family farm or to go West.

Most Americans approved of such decisions. The Horatio Alger heroes rarely held advanced academic degrees. In every machine shop and executive suite at the turn of the century stories were swapped about the kid who went to college, learned a lot of hifalutin theory and then made a mess of his first job.

Lord Palmerston, the British statesman, once said of Cornelius Vanderbilt that it was a pity a man of his ability had not had the advantage of formal schooling. When a friend passed this on to Vanderbilt, the latter snapped, "You tell Lord Palmerston from me that if I had learned education I would not have had time to learn anything else." [8]

At the turn of the century it was assumed that the only fields which required advanced training were medicine, law, the ministry and the scholarly fields, and even in those fields the requirements were exceedingly flexible. Only a tiny proportion of leaders in other fields could boast college degrees.

Despite the foresight of men such as William James, the critical importance of human resources in modern society did not force itself to public attention until very recently, when the nation began to experience dramatic shortages in strategic professions such as medicine, teaching, engineering and physics.

As each profession faced shortages, each laid cool and aggressive plans to capture a bigger share of the oncoming stream of talent. Then it became apparent that the total stream was limited, and studies were initiated to determine whether we were making proper use of our human resources.

The studies revealed that we were making very poor use of these resources and that there was inefficiency and waste in our whole approach to the development of talent. The problems which came to light are not ones which we shall solve easily. Many bright young people do not continue their schooling; others are being ill-trained. Too high a proportion of Negro children grow up in circumstances which are such as to smother talent rather than to nourish it. We make wholly inadequate use of the talents of women in our society.

The educational reforms of the past few years have tackled some of these problems fairly effectively, and others ineffectively. The reforms will continue. Our kind of society must make maximum use of the talent available. It needs desperately to find and train able individuals at many levels, and to an increasing degree modern educational systems are designed to accomplish that result. To the extent that they are not well fitted to achieve that end, they are not modern.

As a result, today's student faces problems of which his great-grandfather never dreamed. He knows that his aptitudes and performance are being measured and predicted from the early grades of school. Every day's performance contributes its score to the inexorable summation that will decide his fate. He sees the brightest youngsters move into the most desirable colleges. He sees industry's recruiters on the college campus asking for the A and B students. He sees the able youngsters heading off into the best jobs. Don't try to tell him how tough it was in the old days. Grandpa had it easy.

Vestiges of Stratification

One of the obstacles to the full development of talent in our society is that we still have not achieved full equality of opportunity.

In stratified societies, the amount of education received by a child depended upon his status in the society. If he was born to rank and wealth he had access to a good education. If he was born in the lower strata he usually did not. In this way, the educational system confirmed and held in place differences in status which were hereditarily determined. Thus was the class war, as well as other wars, won on the playing fields of Eton.

The history of American education has been one long campaign to get as far away from that kind of system as effort and ingenuity could take us. "Geniuses will be raked from the rubbish . . ." wrote Thomas Jefferson.[4] But despite the efforts of generations of Americans to nullify the principle of stratification in our educational system, it still has a good deal of vitality. Most of the obvious positive steps toward true equality of opportunity have been taken; yet major inequalities of opportunity stemming from birth remain. And it will be a formidable task to eradicate these. Being born a Negro, for example, involves obvious limitations on educational opportunity in some parts of the country, and less obvious limitations in *all* parts of the country.

Despite our system of free schools, poverty can still be a profound handicap and wealth a clear advantage. The families at the lowest economic level must all too often live in a slum or near-slum area where the schools do not attract the best teachers. The prosperous citizen can afford a house in an expensive suburb which has a fine school. The good suburban schools are sociologically not unlike the good independent prep schools. The chief difference is that in the suburb, establishing residence is a part—and a very expensive part—of the price of admission (the other part being heavy school taxes). In a way the private prep school is more democratic because it takes in a number of scholarship students of truly impoverished parents. There is no possibility of such an arrangement in Scarsdale. A youngster cannot attend the Scarsdale schools unless his parents live in Scarsdale; and that is something that impoverished parents do not commonly do.

Some of the problems associated with poverty are well illustrated in a case which was brought to my attention several years ago. When Tom B. was a senior in high school, the principal told him his grades were high enough to get him to a good college. Tom took a job in an aircraft factory instead. The principal couldn't understand it, but most of Tom's family and friends would not have understood any other decision. Tom's father, an invalid whose own education ended with the fourth grade, was genuinely—if profanely—proud of Tom's attainments ("The kid talks like a ——— dictionary!"), but thought the boy was already overeducated. His mother, a clerk in the five-and-ten, liked the idea of his going to college but needed his help to support the family. The wages offered by the factory looked like a fortune to Tom. He had worked part time since he was eight, but this was a man's job for a man's pay. He took it.

Actually, poverty is usually accompanied by other complicating factors, and this was so in Tom's case. If he had had a fierce determination to go on to college, he might have found a way. But his diet was deficient in other things besides money. There were virtually no books in Tom's home. No one ever talked about ideas. No one ever mentioned educational goals. Most of Tom's pals in the run-down part of town where he lived had quit school long since. He had literally never had an informal out-of-school chat with anyone who reminisced about his own college years or recommended college to him. It is not surprising, then, that he had no awareness of what college could mean, no motivation to use his fine mind, no aspirations that involved intellectual performance. The image of a fat pay check from the aircraft company was very real; and the image of college was very pale.

Only in recent years have we come to the realization that these deficiencies are as damaging as any monetary handicap. The son of the city's leading lawyer had financial resources that Tom did not have; but even more important, he had an awareness of intellectual values and educational goals. This awareness was passed on to him as a hereditary advantage—in much the same way that money and a title of nobility are passed on. Jacques Barzun says:

There is no mystery about it: the child who is familiar with books, ideas, conversation—the ways and means of the intellectual life—before he begins school, indeed, before he begins consciously to think, has a marked advantage. He is at home in the House of Intellect just as the stableboy is at home among horses, or the child of actors on the stage.[5]

Differences in educational opportunity will never be completely eradicated, but they must be reduced in scope and significance. Americans rightly resent the disparities of social background and the prejudices which limit the recognition of talent wherever it occurs. They will continue to do so as long as such disparities and prejudices exist.

But it would be wrong to leave the impression that stratification of educational opportunity is still a dominant feature of our system. It is not. The vestiges of stratification still exist, but the great drama of American education has been the democratization of educational opportunity over the past century. This has been one of the great social revolutions. In emphasizing that much ground remains to be won, we must not belittle the victories already achieved.

The Market for Talent

We have said that talent is very much in demand in our own society today. But it is not in demand in all societies today. It was not always in demand in our own society. And not all kinds of talent are in demand at any one time.

An earnest young student from a South Asian country said to me, "You talk of the need for education in underdeveloped societies, but my problem is to find a job when I get back. Half my friends are unemployed intellectuals."

His problem is not unique. Part of the difficulty is that his country does not have the broad base of education at lower levels which makes a modern society possible. The young men they send abroad receive first-class modern educations, and come back to a society which is not prepared to use their talents.

Another difficulty is that the fields in which these young men are educated are often chosen without regard to the needs of the society. In some Latin-American countries, for example, very large numbers of young men do the fashionable and traditional thing of preparing themselves in law, even though the last thing their country may need is another lawyer. Similarly in many underdeveloped countries the urge toward industrialization leads more young men into engineering than a pre-industrial society could possibly support.

But the greatest problem is the view taken by the educated man in these countries that his education fits him for (and entitles him to) a job at a certain level of prestige. If such a job is not available, he will often refuse to work. He will not put his superior knowledge to work on whatever tasks the society requires. He does not want to dirty his hands. A European living in Guatemala once said, "There will always be opportunities for able foreigners in this country—as long as the best-educated Guatemalans refuse to live outside the capital city."

It was once widely believed in this country that there would never be more than a limited market for educated talent. As recently as the

1930's, learned treatises were being written to warn against the overproduction of highly educated people. One still hears echoes of this theme. But in recent years we have reached a stage of development in which these fears have less basis. The demand is so great that there is little likelihood of unemployment of highly trained people.

But even in our own society there may be overproduction of educated talent in specific lines. Indeed, on many occasions in the future there will be an imbalance between the number of men trained for a given line of work and the number of jobs available. Attempts will be made to minimize this through accurate forecasts of manpower needs, but experience with such forecasts has been discouraging. The alternative— and the wiser course—is to educate men and women who are capable of applying excellent fundamental training to a wide range of specific jobs.

Nothing contributes more damagingly to the unemployment of educated talent than rigid specialization and rigid attitudes supporting this specialization. The future is necessarily hazardous for the individual who trains himself to do a specific job, receives an advanced degree for that line of work and believes that society owes him a living doing it. If technological innovations reduce the demand for his specialty, he has nowhere to go. On the other hand, if he is broadly trained in fundamental principles, and knows that he may have to apply those principles in varying contexts over the years, he is in a position to survive the ups and downs of the job market.

There has been a curious shift in the nature of our anxieties concerning the lower end of the spectrum of ability. For many years, when we were steadily upgrading the lower strata of society in terms of literacy and conditions of life, thoughtful people were inclined to say, "This is all very well, but when everyone gets educated, who's going to do the dirty work?" That is a rather old-fashioned question today. There has been a dramatic reduction in the amount of "dirty work" in our society, and we are paying quite high wages for the dirty work that remains. The fear now is that automation may reduce unskilled jobs so substantially that there will be serious unemployment. This leads to some interesting social questions, but they are not ones which we can explore in this context.

Although a modern society is wise to foster talent on as wide a scale as possible, no society, modern or traditional, can promise every talented individual the opportunity to earn a living in the exercise of his talent. Some years ago I wrote an article describing the need for talent in modern society and shortly thereafter received an aggrieved letter from a correspondent who described his own talent along a certain line and asserted that he could not market it. He believed that society owed him a living for the exercise of this talent, and he was deeply embittered by the treatment he had received.

But the truth is that no society will ever provide a living for every kind of talent. We need not dwell on the fact that some kinds of talent —for picking pockets, let us say—have to be discouraged; nor that other kinds—the capacity to imitate birdcalls, for example—are trivial. Even in the case of genuinely important gifts— the gifts of the artist, writer, composer, architect or sculptor—the individual can never assume that society will support him in the exercise of his talent. Talent is one thing and the marketability of talent is something else. The latter will depend upon the kind and degree of talent involved, the attitudes of society toward that talent, the prosperity of the society and many other things. It will never be easy for the gifted individual who is ahead of his time (or behind the times) or who exercises his talent in a way that does not coincide with the fashion of the moment.

Talented young people should not be misled in these matters. They must not be led to assume that there is always a market for talent. But while the individual must be realistic, all who care about excellence in a society must be vigilant concerning the waste of talent. Teachers, curators, deans, critics, art dealers, editors, foundation officers, publishers—in short, all who are in a position to encourage talent—should continuously ask themselves whether the society

is providing sufficient opportunities for its varied
resources of talent. If important kinds of talent
are withering on the vine, they had better know
why.

chapter V

The Identification of Talent

"My boy is something of a genius," said the Scarsdale commuter to his seat companion on the 5:26 P.M. train. He wasn't speaking metaphorically, he wasn't joking and he wasn't consciously boasting. He said it in a matter-of-fact way, as he might have said, "My boy has a pet hamster." After pausing long enough to let his companion express a decent interest, he went on to report the basis for his judgment—the very high scores his youngster had made on a scholastic aptitude test.

Geniuses used to be rare. Today, thanks to popular interpretation of test scores, every elementary or secondary school has its quota.

The chief instrument used in the search for talent is the standardized test. It would be surprising if the tests were not the object of considerable hostility. They have been. They are unpopular for a number of reasons.

Many people have an aversion to being the subject of mental diagnosis. In some this aversion to the tests is defensive: they fear precise appraisal of their own (or their children's) capacities. In others the aversion is simply a normal reaction to what they consider an invasion of privacy.

Many fear that the tests will be inaccurate—that they will come up with an appraisal of Johnny that isn't fair to Johnny's talents. The fact that the tests may have high statistical reliability and validity does not quiet this apprehension. A neighbor of mine, an investment banker, said, "They tell me the tests are right 95 per cent of the time, but suppose my Billy is in the remaining 5 per cent?"

Apprehension is fostered by the fact that it is very hard for those without professional training in psychology to understand the processes of mental measurement. No one wishes to be judged by a process he cannot comprehend.

To some degree, fear of the tests is a fear of the potentialities for social manipulation and control inherent in any large-scale processing of individuals. The tests bring vividly to mind the hazards of a society which deals with the individual as a statistic. The investment banker quoted earlier put it this way: "I just resist the idea that my boy's life can be changed by a mark made electronically on a slip of paper a thousand miles away by an anonymous person or machine, acting on criteria unknown to me, and using a measuring instrument I can't comprehend." In short, there is not only fear of the tests but fear of the unknown bureaucracy which handles the testing and acts on the results.

No one concerned with the future of testing

can afford to ignore these sources of anxiety. On the other hand, even if these sources of concern were to disappear, the hostility toward the tests would probably remain. *The tests are designed to do an unpopular job.* An untutored observer listening to critics lash out at the imperfections of the tests might suppose that the criticisms would be stilled if the tests were perfected. Not at all. As the tests improve and become less vulnerable to present criticism, the hostility to them may actually increase. A proverbial phrase indicating complete rejection is, "I wouldn't like it even if it were good." With the tests, the more appropriate phrase might be, "I wouldn't like them *especially* if they were good."

As a matter of fact some of the tests are excellent even today—within the limits for which they were designed. The development of standardized tests is one of the great success stories in the objective study of human behavior. Anyone who understands the problems of mental measurement must be impressed with the technical achievement these instruments represent.

It is now objected that the tests give an advantage to the individual of good family background and place the individual of poor background at a disadvantage. This is true in some measure. But it must never be forgotten that the tests introduced an objectivity into the measurement of human abilities that never before existed. Before the tests were developed a great many people seriously believed that the less-educated segments of society were not *capable* of being educated. And the view is still prevalent in many societies.

An acquaintance of mine who recently visited a provincial school in France reported, "The teacher seemed to find it impossible to separate his judgment of a pupil's intelligence from his judgment of the pupil's cleanliness, good manners, neatness of dress and precision of speech. Needless to say, his students from the upper and upper middle social classes excelled in these qualities." Before the rise of objective tests American teachers were susceptible—at least in some degree—to the same social distortion of judgment. Against this background, modern methods of mental measurement hit the educational system like a fresh breeze. The tests couldn't see whether the youngster was in rags or in tweeds, and they couldn't hear the accents of the slum. The tests revealed intellectual gifts at every level of the population.

This is not to say that the tests completely eliminate unfair advantage for the young person of privileged social background. They do not. But they are more fair than any method previously used.

Anyone attacking the usefulness of the tests must suggest workable alternatives. It has been proved over and over again that the alternative methods of evaluating ability are subject to gross errors and capable of producing grave injustices. Whatever their faults, the tests have proven fairer and more reliable than any other method when they are used cautiously within the limits for which they were designed.

The best achievement and aptitude tests are remarkably effective in sorting out students according to their actual and potential performance in the classroom. But even in this context they are far from perfect, and any system of identification of talent which assumes them to be perfect will commit grave mistakes.

Of all mistakes made in using the tests, perhaps the worst are made in trying to apply the results beyond the strictly academic or intellectual performances for which the tests were designed. Such mistakes occur for quite understandable reasons. The scholastic aptitude and achievement tests are almost the only really effective tests we have. Everyone knows that there are other powerful ingredients in successful performance—attitudes, values, motives, non-academic talents—but we have no reliable way of measuring these other ingredients. The temptation is almost overwhelming to lean too heavily on the effective—but limited—measures we do possess.

This error produces grievous difficulties when we try to identify young people who will exhibit high performance in later life. Performance in later life places heavy emphasis on precisely those attributes not measured by scholastic aptitude and achievement tests. The youth who has these unmeasurable traits—e.g., zeal, judgment, staying power—to a high degree may not be identified in school as a person of high potential but may enjoy marked success in later life. Similarly, the young person extremely high on scholastic attributes which the tests can measure but lacking in other attributes required by success in life may prove to be a "morning glory."

Anyone who has spent his life around colleges can cite many examples of such apparent (but not necessarily real) shifts in potential. They are usually not nearly so perplexing as we pretend. Many years ago a talented youngster named Rennie D. was brought to my attention by his fond mother. Rennie was a gifted child of the most readily identifiable sort. He was extremely articulate, extremely quick in schoolwork. He was also lazy, self-indulgent, flaccid and infantile in his emotions and personality; but these didn't interfere with his school performance. He was good-looking in a clean, open, pudgy way, and teachers loved him not only for his brightness but for his amiability. He sailed through school and college and graduated *magna cum laude,* as his mother assured me he would. But in the twenty years since then he hasn't done a blessed thing.

We like to say that this is puzzling, but in fact it is not. Scholastic aptitude is a central ingredient in school performance and Rennie had it to a high degree. But there are other crucial ingredients in adult performance and apparently he lacked them.

Fortunately, such cases are rare. The "early bloom, early fade" pattern is not common. Most youngsters who show early gifts bear out their promise in some measure. But Rennie is a vivid reminder that the tests were not designed to test success in life.

We now know enough about the tests to suggest rules for minimizing the hazards and maximizing the benefits of these instruments.

By all odds the most important rule is that the tests should not be the sole reliance in identifying talent. Judgments of the youngster's aptitudes and achievements should be based on many kinds of evidence. The tests are one kind of evidence. School grades are another kind. The teachers' written judgments of the student represent another kind of evidence. The judgments of deans, principals and counselors who have had dealings with the child may be useful. The important thing to be borne in mind is that every known measure of aptitudes and achievements has some failings. Only by drawing upon a considerable variety of evidence can we be certain that our judgment is well-rounded and fair to the young person.

An equally important rule is that diagnosis of the young person's aptitudes and achievements must be a continuing process. It is not enough to say that the child has been tested. Has he been tested lately? Has he been tested consistently over the years? We should no more

accept a test score that is several years old than
we would accept a health report that is several
years old. It would be misleading to suggest that
repeated testings must be made because we expect major variations in the youngster's aptitudes
from year to year. The truth is that his aptitudes
will probably remain pretty stable. But at any
given age level, a test score may not be a precise
reflection of his aptitude. The test used that
year may not have been a good one. The score
may have been inaccurately calculated. Or it
may have been inaccurately recorded. The same
requirement of repetition is relevant in the case
of school grades and all the other measures on
which a judgment is to be based. Any one of
them may have been less than accurate in a particular year, and repeated appraisals correct such
inaccuracies. And quite aside from inaccuracies
in appraisal, the student himself may change
from year to year—if not in aptitude then in
achievement, in motivation and in many of the
other dimensions on which judgments are necessarily based.

Still another important rule is that crucial
judgments on the youngster's future should not
be based entirely on intellectual gifts. We have
pointed out that traits of personality and character are of central importance in the child's
later performance. And there are many kinds of
socially valuable talent—e.g., in art and music
—which are not measured by the tests. All of
these should carry due weight in any decisions

which are made. This is so obvious that one might wonder why it needs to be mentioned—but the plain fact is that the easiest, laziest thing to do is to sort youngsters out by their scholastic aptitude scores and forget the complications. Teachers should not only combat this laziness; they should actively seek out other dimensions of talent, they should be constantly on the alert for the other attributes that promise to strengthen and guide performance in later life.

The sorting out of individuals in a society is an exceedingly serious business—and a potentially explosive one. No stone should be left unturned to insure that decisions are based on a wide range of evidence, carefully gathered and sifted. And precisely because the consequences for the individual are so serious, the final weighing of evidence, the final judgment that puts it all together, must be made by a qualified and responsible human being rather than by a machine. With all the rich evidence of human fallibility, with all the folk wisdom about human errors in judgment, people still insist that the final decisions concerning their fate be made by their fellow humans.

Diagnosis of an individual's future capacity to perform remains a hazardous undertaking. There are mysteries in individual development which we are far from understanding. Through repeated appraisals of the youngster at various ages, through the use of a variety of measures, through the pooling of many judgments, we are simply acknowledging the complexity of the subject and proceeding with the caution which that complexity dictates.

And it cannot be emphasized too often that the greatest enemy of such caution is the apparent simplicity and efficiency involved in assigning a single number to each youngster. The rapid and efficient handling of large numbers of individuals exerts tremendous pressure toward oversimplified diagnoses, toward the summation of individual attributes in a single index number and toward complete dependence on that number as a key to the individual's fate. Considerations of efficiency must not be allowed to falsify our diagnoses nor to narrow our conception of talent.

chapter VI

Facts and Fancies about Talent

The strategy a society adopts in dealing with differences in ability may depend in part on its views concerning the hereditary nature of such differences. As we shall see, the genetic facts cannot be wholly decisive for social policy. But in the past, certain widely held views concerning heredity have played a powerful role in buttressing social policy with respect to differences in ability.

In societies of hereditary privilege it is usually widely believed that the social strata correspond to hereditary differences in human quality. The society is stratified, the argument runs, because people do differ in quality; and since these differences are hereditary, the stratification is hereditary. This view is most strongly held by the upper classes of a stratified society, of course, but it is apt to be partially accepted throughout the society. It is always startling to the American traveling in a stratified society to discover that though the lower classes may resent certain social inequalities, they more than half accept the ideology that supports those inequalities. I recall

the astonishment of a young American soldier in
Italy in 1944 when an elderly Italian servant
patiently explained to him that the social hierarchy was based on the unshakable facts of
human heredity.

The democracies, of course, officially rejected
the idea that differences in social status were due
to differences in hereditary quality. But even in
the democracies the notion refused to die. Her-
bert Spencer, for example, believed that the poor
were "unfit" and should be eliminated. Criticiz-
ing this view, Henry George once wrote:

Mr. Spencer is like one who might insist that each
should swim for himself in crossing a river, ignoring the
fact that some had been artificially provided with corks
and others artificially loaded with lead.[1]

But Mr. Spencer's view of the unfitness of the
poor did not die. It was too tempting for the
rich and wellborn to suppose that the stratification existing at any given moment was rooted in
enduring human qualities. It was too easy to
imagine that the latest crop of immigrants was
humanly incapable of rising from ignorance and
poverty. Thus H. G. Wells wrote in 1906:

I doubt very much if America is going to assimilate
all that she is taking in now; much more do I doubt
that she will assimilate the still greater inflow of the
coming years. . . . I believe that if things go on as they
are going, the great mass of them will remain a very
low lower class—will remain largely illiterate industrialized peasants.[2]

The view that the social strata coincided with a natural hierarchy of ability received a shattering blow with the development of relatively objective measures of mental performance. The earliest wide-scale use of objective tests, in World War I, made it clear that intelligence was broadly distributed in the population and that there were rich resources of ability at every social level.

Though the tests made it clear that mental performance did not follow the lines of social stratification, they did not settle the question of whether ability was hereditary. For years this was one of the liveliest topics of debate among research people in psychology.

It is sufficiently controversial as a purely intellectual question; it becomes more so because of its implications for social theory. The argument quickly takes on political overtones. Individuals whose weighing of the evidence leads them to believe that heredity is the dominant factor in intelligence find that this conclusion endears them to some conservative elements in the society, and gains the hostility of certain left-wing thinkers. Lewis Terman was bitterly criticized by the Communists for placing what they considered to be too much emphasis on heredity and too little on environment in the determination of the IQ. On the other hand, the individual whose weighing of the evidence persuades him that environment is more important than heredity finds himself applauded by some liberals who want very much to believe that the intellectual inequalities between men are due to social inequalities.

It is not easy to settle an intellectual question when people have a powerful emotional stake in one or another outcome. As a matter of fact, the experts have long since concluded that for most purposes the question is neither profitable nor meaningful. They point out that it is simply unreal to ask how much of behavior is determined by heredity and how much by environment as though one were asking how many eggs and how much milk went into a pudding. The question oversimplifies an enormously complex matter and treats as separate and self-contained ingredients two factors which are essentially inseparable.

But the layman is not concerned to achieve clarity in matters of theory. He wants to know what it all means for him and for his child. And the truth is that most experts are in reasonable agreement (though they would never admit it) as to what it means for him.

It is clear, for example, that the striking differences in environment that exist do have some effect upon intellectual performance. One youngster may find himself in a stimulating and instructive environment from the first days of infancy. Intelligent adults may give him immeasurable help in learning the names of objects, understanding the consequences of acts and seeing the connections between things. An environment rich in toys, pictures, books and responsive people may give him abundant opportunities for learning and for broadening his horizon. The next child may have a barren and impoverished environment, little or no attention from parents or other children and no tutoring at all in the simple lessons of childhood.

There is evidence that such differences do affect intelligence as measured by tests. But there is also ample evidence that the effect of environmental circumstances on test performance is rather limited. This has been demonstrated in studies of identical twins reared apart. It is also suggested by the relative stability of the IQ. If environmental circumstances powerfully affect the IQ, one would not expect the IQ to be a very stable measure. The IQ is far from constant —it can be affected in a variety of ways by environmental factors, and in any substantial batch of cases it is possible to point to some fairly marked changes in individual IQs over a period of years. But considering the wide range of environments through which human beings pass, the remarkable thing about the IQ is its relative stability.

The precise degree of stability of intelligence, as measured by tests, is the subject of considerable debate among some of the experts. But the majority of modern workers in the field have a balanced view of the question. They recognize the relative stability of intelligence, but they are willing to accord ample weight to environmental influences.

When we examine the appropriate social policy to be adopted in the light of these findings, we are faced with a simpler task than the behavior theorists are faced with. For purposes of social policy, precise answers on this question are not necessary. Even if environment were a modest factor in determining intelligence, social policy would necessarily emphasize the importance of taking this factor into account. Even if only one child in ten could gain in intellectual effectiveness through a more favorable environment, we would still be bound to make the effort.

The other major factor in social policy must be a straightforward admission of the fact that individuals do differ greatly in their capacities, and each must be enabled to develop the talent that is in him. *Whether individual differences in ability are innate or are due to environmental differences, we must deal with them imaginatively and constructively.*

If we are going to develop a sensible approach to the encouragement of talent, we shall have to dispose of a good many myths surrounding the talented individual.

One such myth is summoned up in the phrase "early bloom, early fade." There is an old wives' tale to the effect that most highly gifted children "burn themselves out" and never amount to anything as adults. The companion belief is that great men were almost invariably either dull or fractious children. Neither is true.

There is something immensely satisfying about both beliefs and it is a pity to explode them. What could be more comforting to ordinary mortals than the thought that Winston Churchill was an unpromising youngster? Or that Charles Darwin had trouble in school? Or that William Faulkner was a poor student? But it has been demonstrated over and over that youngsters who show early promise tend to perform better in later life than youngsters who do not show early promise.

And research on the early careers of people of great ability has demonstrated that as a rule their gifts were observable even in childhood. Alexander Pope was twelve years old—junior high school age in this country—when he penned the melancholy lines,

> Thus let me live unseen, unknown,
> Thus unlamented let me die,
> Steal from the world, and not a stone
> Tell where I lie.

Mozart learned to play the clavier between three and four years of age. Carlyle was only eleven months old and had never spoken a word when, hearing another child in the household cry, he sat up and said, "What ails wee Jock?" [3] A great many such examples could be listed.

There are, of course, plenty of exceptions. And there should be. Success involves more than talent, and some individuals simply lack the character or motivation to make the most of their talent. A professor said of one of my more indolent classmates, "He has great gifts but he's too lazy to unwrap them." Similarly, some youngsters who will exhibit greatness in later life fail to reveal their gifts early. But on the whole, talent is by no means the capricious thing that legend would have it. Promise is usually borne out. The classic research in this field is of course the work of Lewis Terman, who selected a group of 1,000 gifted children for long-term study. The study has been going on for approximately 40 years now, and the evidence of continued high performance is impressive.

Another popular misconception is the notion that great talent is usually highly specific. We tend to assume that the man of extremely high talent is narrowly gifted. But the research evidence indicates that gifted individuals generally have many talents rather than a single talent. If the individual is promising in one line, the best guess is that he will be promising in a number of lines.

He probably will not develop his gifts along all the lines open to him, so in later life he may seem less broadly talented than he actually is. Some narrowing is inevitable. There are limitations of time and energy. And there is a "tyranny of talent" which tends to force the narrowing of anyone with extraordinarily high ability in a specific line. Once the talent is discovered it is often so highly rewarded that the individual is apt to neglect (or not to discover) his other talents; and society abets him in this neglect. With all those clavichord recitals at age seven, Mozart could not have had much time for exploration of his other gifts. Such one-sided development may be essential to the highest reaches of performance, and it might be foolish to try to prevent it in people of great talent. But anyone responsible for very gifted young people would do well to assist them in exploring the full range of their talents where possible, and to postpone at least for a time the tyrannical narrowing down.

Still another misconception concerning talented individuals is that they are indecisive, impractical, unreliable in positions of responsibility, and unfit for active life. This is certainly not true of talented people generally. As a matter of fact, large numbers of highly talented individuals choose managerial or other "practical" activities as the chief outlet for their talents. And even those who choose more cloistered paths are not necessarily forced to do so by their own limitations. During World War II many gifted scholars proved themselves extremely able administrators in emergency assignments. And it is a fallacy, in any case, to suppose that responsibility, decisiveness and judgment are qualities which can be tested only in the market place. It is true that the decisions involved in a normal business day might be torture to the average professor, but it is equally true that the decisions involved in composing a lecture would be torture to the average business executive. And the practical realities of faculty politics would test the shrewdness of a congressional party whip.

This is not to say that there is nothing to the legendary impracticality of the talented individual. There are certain fields—art and music, for example—in which society encourages the individual of great gifts to be impractical, and many individuals accept that invitation. But this may be a culturally determined trait. If they lived in a society which defined great artists as highly practical, they might well be so.

Still another myth is that the extremely gifted individual is unstable. In this case the myth is particularly hard to disprove because of the vivid examples which seem to support it. One thinks of Van Gogh cutting off his ear, of Poe's alcoholism, of Nietzsche's incoherent end. But again, the weight of solid evidence is in the other direction. Whenever systematic data have been gathered on a wide range of gifted individuals it has been found that they are apt to be more stable than the less gifted.

part three

Individual Differences

chapter VII

Education as a Sorting-Out Process

The Rigors of Sorting Out

Every school morning some 42 million American children gulp their breakfast, grab their books, slam the front door and dash off to class. Among them go not one but several future presidents of the United States, a handful of future Supreme Court justices and dozens of future cabinet members.

We have talked about how our society deals with differences in ability. There is no better place to observe this process than the educational system.

We have also talked about the extent to which ability determines the individual's status in life. Educational systems have always had a great deal to do with the eventual status of the individuals who pass through them. It was said of German university students at the end of the nineteenth century that one-third broke down, one-third went to the devil, and the remaining third went on to govern Europe.

Americans believe that ability should be recognized at whatever level in society it occurs.

They like to think that those future presidents dashing off to school may come from any walk of life.

But as education becomes increasingly effective in pulling the bright youngster to the top, it becomes an increasingly rugged sorting-out process for everyone concerned. This is true today and it will be very much more so in the future. The schools are the golden avenue of opportunity for able youngsters; but by the same token they are the arena in which less able youngsters discover their limitations. This thought rarely occurred to the generations of Americans who dreamed of universal education. They saw the beauty of a system in which every young person could go as far as his ability and ambition would take him, without obstacles of money, social standing, religion or race. They didn't reflect on the pain involved for those who lacked the necessary ability. Yet pain there is and must be.

Although the American people have never explicitly faced up to the realities of the sorting-out process, they have demonstrated in many ways that they sense the painfulness of it. It will be worth our while to consider some examples of American practice on this point.

Even the most casual glance at our educational system will reveal our great reluctance to put labels on individual differences in general capacity. Consider the broad interpretation we give to the phrase "college education." When young people are graduated from high school we discuss those going on to college as though they were a homogeneous lot, all headed for a similar experience. But the truth is that they are quietly but fairly effectively sorted into different paths.

Anyone who has enjoyed a behind-the-scenes view of how a good high school deals with its graduating seniors is familiar with the process. Consider the work of Miss L., assistant principal in an Eastern high school. One of her tasks is to advise the girls who want to go on to college. Miss L. has a clear impression of every girl in the senior class. She has known most of them since they entered high school. She knows what subjects they like and what subjects they find easy. She knows how hard they work and what their hopes are for college. And she knows a great deal about colleges—what the entrance requirements are, and what kind of girl is apt to be happy in what college.

The students need not listen to Miss L.'s advice but usually do. She sends her college-bound girls out along widely diverging pathways—to colleges of the highest possible standards, to colleges of moderate difficulty and so on down to colleges which may actually be lower academically than the best high schools. But though she must appraise accurately the relative standings of colleges and the relative capacities of students, Miss L. will usually not make these appraisals explicit. She will not say bluntly that the student is of limited intelligence and therefore should go to a second-class college. She will tell the parents that their youngster is not "a natural student" or "not one of those with a tremendous drive to get grades" and therefore should probably go to one of the colleges "where the entrance requirements are not quite so exacting."

Dr. and Mrs. Roger Barker, American psychologists, recently made an intensive study of the daily lives of children in the small town of Leyburn, England. One of the many striking differences they found between Leyburn and a comparable American town was the degree of candor about differences in ability. In England when a school child gave a foolish answer the teacher was likely to respond with a candid appraisal of his performance and even of his native capacity. It was not at all unthinkable for the teacher to make some remark such as, "Johnny, sit down—you're not up to this." [1]

Such candor is outside the experience of most American observers. The American teacher might say that Johnny had not studied his lesson, or that Johnny was lazy, or that Johnny was inattentive. She might impugn his cooperativeness, or his ambition, or his knowledge. But she would rarely indicate that his ability was limited. We much prefer not to discuss such matters at all. Indeed we are capable of devising rather elaborate institutional arrangements to get around the necessity of telling Johnny that he is at the low end of the distribution of ability.

One point of view to take toward this national

peculiarity is that it is nonsensical and that we have developed a ridiculous squeamishness about such matters. Critics trace it to our desire to make children "happy," to our concern for psychological adjustment. But such critics are barking up the wrong tree. The reason we do not like to label differences in capacity is that individual capacity holds a uniquely important place in our scheme of things.

It must never be forgotten that ours is one of the few societies in the history of the world in which performance is a primary determinant of status. What the individual can "deliver" in the way of performance is a major factor in how far he can rise in the world. In a stratified society, performance is not an important factor in establishing the individual's status, so he can afford to be less deeply concerned about his capacity. For every step that a society takes away from a stratified system and toward a system in which performance is the chief determinant of status, the individual will be increasingly concerned about his capacity. In our society the individual's future depends to an unprecedented degree on his own gifts.

There are all kinds of individual capacity. That is a point to which we shall return. But for complex reasons, Americans see appraisals of "intelligence," however defined, as total judgments on the individual and as central to his self-esteem. Some critics note that we discriminate nicely between excellence and mediocrity in athletics, but refuse to be similarly precise about differences in intelligence; and they attribute this to the fact that we are more seriously concerned with athletic ability than we are with intelligence. Nothing could be farther from the truth. We can afford, emotionally speaking, to be coldly objective in judgments of athletic ability precisely because we do not take these as total judgments on the individual or as central to his self-esteem.

Another feature of our dealing with levels of ability is what I shall call our principle of multiple chances. The European system separates youngsters at ten or eleven years of age on the basis of ability, and begins preparing some for university education, others for less demanding levels of education. This is in many respects an efficient procedure; and some critics of our schools, such as Admiral Rickover, think it would solve most of our problems. It does avoid some of the problems which plague our comprehensive high schools. But in the American view, it presents a host of difficulties, only one of which need be noted here: early separation of the very gifted and the less gifted violates our principle of multiple chances.

We believe that the youngster should have many successive opportunities to discover himself. We postpone as long as possible any final closing of the door on the individual's chances. It is a unique feature of our system that the "late bloomer" may dawdle or occupy himself with other than educational objectives until as late as eighteen or nineteen years of age (roughly first or second year of college) and still (provided that he is able) not only obtain a college education but go on to become a professional man.

Not long ago a friend in a Western city mentioned a Dr. S. to me, and described him as "the best internist in town." The name was familiar and I asked if he were the S. who had attended the University of California in the 1930's. He was. But the image that my memory supplied was not that of a brilliant pre-med student. It was of a pleasantly aimless young man with no interest in studies and no goal more serious than to hold his position as shortstop on the baseball team. I mentioned this to my friend, and he grinned. "That was S. all right; but in his junior year he woke up, and after that nothing could stop him."

That is the sort of story we all find pleasing, but it should not mislead us. It is rare for aimless young men with no interest in studies to turn into leading physicians. And S. was fortunate to have graduated from high school thirty years ago. Today he would have much greater difficulty getting in (and staying in) a good university, and far greater trouble getting in a good medical school. Even a very prosperous society cannot afford to spend large sums allowing such youngsters to loaf their way through a prolonged adolescence.

It is not only the late bloomer who benefits

by the principle of multiple chances. We now know beyond any doubt that the social and cultural influences of the home have a good deal to do with both motivation and performance in school. The child growing up in a home barren of educational or cultural influences may require a longer exposure to school before he wakes up.

The practice followed by many of our public universities of accepting all high school graduates who apply and then weeding them out in large numbers during freshman year is partly a response to political pressures. But it is also warmly defended by many in terms of our principle of multiple chances. It can be argued that it is better to let a student try and fail—and in failing discover his own inadequacy—than to tell him he is not good enough to try. Of course, the answer to this would be that the youngster has already had many chances to prove himself before he reaches college. True, says the defender of the system, but the extraordinary symbolic importance which college education is gaining in our society may require that the youngster be given one further try. It can be argued that allowing young people to discover their own inadequacies is a pretty sensible social strategy.

The powerful impulses on the part of the American people to temper the wind to the less able youngsters make the critics of American education grind their teeth in despair. And their despair is not wholly unjustified. But no one has a right to join the critics until he has thought long and hard about the authentic difficulty of the social problem which the American system must solve. The sorting out of individuals according to ability is very nearly the most delicate and difficult process our society has to face.

Those who receive the most education are going to move into virtually all the key jobs. Thus the question "Who should go to college?" translates itself into the more compelling question "Who is going to manage the society?" That is not the kind of question one can treat lightly or cavalierly. It is the kind of question that wars have been fought over.

It must never be forgotten that a person born to low status in a rigidly stratified society has a far more acceptable self-image than the person who loses out in our free competition of talent. In an older society, the humble member of society can attribute his lowly status to God's will, to the ancient order of things or to a corrupt and tyrannous government. But if a society sorts people out efficiently and fairly according to their gifts, the loser knows that the true reason for his lowly status is that he is not capable of better. That is a bitter pill for any man.

An example may clarify the problem. In the course of World War II, a military commander told me about a situation he had encountered in the small unit under his command. This unit had been organized for special work, and had an unusual number of highly intelligent enlisted men. An opportunity arose to send men to officers' candidate school, and the commander set it as his high-minded goal to recommend every one of his enlisted men who was properly qualified. He screened them, identified those of officer caliber, and every one that he recommended was accepted for officers' candidate school.

What were the consequences? The morale of the remaining enlisted men disintegrated. Investigation revealed that the screening process had left them without a shred of self-esteem. They were relatively happy as long as they could say to themselves that they were enlisted men because this is an unjust world, or because the military services do not value ability. But the commanding officer's scrupulous search for talent had deprived them of those comfortable defenses. They had no place to hide. It was now clear to all concerned that they were enlisted men because that was where they belonged.

This is an instructive parable for those who fail to see the social hazards in rigorous selection of able people. And yet we must engage in such selection. As we shall see, there are ways to do it wisely.

The Hazards of Mediocrity

We have given sufficient emphasis to the painfulness of the sorting-out process. It remains to point out that when we over-react to this painfulness, we tumble into a ditch on the other side of the road. And that ditch is no less deep. At times our desire to protect young people from invidious comparisons has produced serious confusion in educational objectives and a dangerous erosion of standards. Such consequences, whether rare or frequent, are a legitimate cause for concern. Because of the leveling influences which are inevitable in popular government, a democracy must, more than any other form of society, maintain what Ralph Barton Perry has called "an express insistence upon quality and distinction." When it does not do so, the consequences are all too familiar: the deterioration of standards, the debasement of taste, shoddy education, vulgar art, cheap politics and the tyranny of the lowest common denominator,

> Where blind and naked Ignorance
> Delivers brawling judgments, unashamed,
> On all things all day long.[2]

We must face the fact that our kind of society does not always find it easy to applaud the superior individual. It is interesting in this connection to note that some of the best examples of ungrudging tribute to gifted individuals were to be found in societies of hereditary stratification. Such societies ruthlessly suppressed talent in most instances. But once the man of great gifts won recognition, he enjoyed the benefits of a society which had deeply-ingrained habits of rewarding superiority (as it defined superiority).

In efforts to force a spurious equality, we can detect not only the hand of the generous man who honestly regrets that some must lose the foot race, but the hand of the envious man who resents achievement, detests superiority in others and will punish eminence at every opportunity. These latter are the men Henry Becque had in mind when he said, "The defect of equality is that we only desire it with our superiors." [8]

Standards are contagious. They spread throughout an organization, a group or a society. If an organization or group cherishes high standards, the behavior of individuals who enter it is inevitably influenced. Similarly, if slovenliness infects a society, it is not easy for any member of that society to remain uninfluenced in his own behavior. With that grim fact in mind, one is bound to look with apprehension on many segments of our national life in which slovenliness has attacked like dry rot, eating away the solid timber.

Even those who are deeply impressed—as all should be—by the great positive achievements of our schools and colleges over the past century must agree that we have worried all too little about the individual of unusual gifts. This is not to say that we were wrong in giving unprecedented attention to the average youngster. Our kind of society demands the maximum development of individual potentialities *at every level of ability;* and we would be very foolish indeed if we were to let our renewed interest in the gifted youngster lead to neglect of everyone else. Martin Luther said that humanity is like a drunken peasant who is always ready to fall from his horse on one side or the other, and in that respect we Americans are all too human. We must learn to see the achievements and short-comings of our educational system in some sort of embracing perspective which will permit us to repair one defect without creating others.

And the first requirement is that we clear up some of the confusions involved in our handling of individual differences. Consider two statements drawn from recent discussions of individual differences. The first is by a schoolteacher, who says, "I regard it as undemocratic to treat so-called gifted children any differently from other children. To me all children are gifted." The second statement is by a professor of education: "The goal of the American educational system is to enable every youngster to fulfill his potentialities, regardless of his race, creed, social standing or economic position."

The first statement implies that you must treat all children the same. The second insists that we must enable each to fulfill his potentialities. The conflict between the two emerges if it proves impossible to enable each to fulfill his potentialities without treating each differently.

It is the old, old dilemma of equalitarianism. In this case, the professor of education has stated the basic American creed and has left the path open for differential treatment, so that each youngster may achieve the best that is in him, while the schoolteacher has closed off the possibility that each may achieve his best. She might be willing to have each achieve his best provided that it did not require differential treatment. But if it does require differential treatment, she will presumably deny him the opportunity.

The traditional democratic invitation to each individual to achieve the best that is in him requires that we provide each youngster with the particular kind of education which will benefit *him*. That is the only sense in which equality of opportunity can mean anything. The good society is not one that ignores individual differences but one that deals with them wisely and humanely. As William Learned wrote:

The conception of a democratic education as one leveled to a colorless mediocrity is as grotesque an interpretation of democratic principles as [a conception] of health in which abounding vitality . . . is deprecated on the ground that only average health is fair to the community. No one believes this. . . .[4]

chapter VIII

College and the Alternatives

Who Should Go to College

All of the conflicting and confusing notions which Americans have concerning equality, excellence and the encouragement of talent may be observed with crystal clarity in the current discussions of "who should go to college." In the years ahead these discussions will become more heated. Pressure of enrollments will make it far harder to get into the better colleges, and there will be lively debate over who has a "right" to a college education.

A good deal of this debate will center around issues of quality versus quantity in education. Douglas Bush eloquently enunciated one extreme position in the phrase, "Education for all is education for none." [1]

Arguments about quality in higher education tend to be heated and rather pointless. There are many reasons why such conversations become muddled, the foremost being that they so often degenerate into arguments over "elite" versus "mass" education. People who engage in these arguments are like the two washerwomen

Sydney Smith observed leaning out of their back windows and quarreling with each other across the alley: "They could never agree," Smith said, "because they were arguing from different premises." [2] In the case of arguments over "elite" versus "mass" education, I am convinced that both premises should be vacated, because behind the arguments is the assumption that a society must decide whether it wishes to educate a few people exceedingly well *or* to educate a great number of people rather badly.

This is an imaginary dilemma. It is possible to have excellence in education and at the same time to seek to educate everyone to the limit of his ability. A society such as ours has no choice but to seek the development of human potentialities at all levels. It takes more than an educated elite to run a complex, technological society. Every modern, industrialized society is learning that hard lesson.

The notion that so-called quality education and so-called mass education are mutually exclusive is woefully out of date. It would not have survived at all were there not a few remarkably archaic characters in our midst. We all know that some of the people calling most noisily for quality in education are those who were *never* reconciled to the widespread extension of educational opportunity. To such individuals there is something inherently vulgar about large numbers of people. At the other extreme are the fanatics who believe that the chief goal for

higher education should be to get as many
youngsters as possible—regardless of ability—
into college classrooms. Such individuals regard
quality as a concept smacking faintly of Louis
XIV.

But neither extreme speaks for the American
people, and neither expresses the true issues that
pose themselves today. It would be fatal to allow
ourselves to be tempted into an anachronistic
debate. *We must seek excellence in a context
of concern for all.* A democracy, no less than any
other form of society, must foster excellence if it
is to survive; and it should not allow the emotional scars of old battles to confuse it on this
point.

Educating everyone up to the limit of his
ability does not mean sending everyone to college. Part of any final answer to the college
problem must be some revision of an altogether
false emphasis which the American people are
coming to place on college education. This false
emphasis is the source of great difficulties for us.
In Virginia they tell the story of the kindly
Episcopal minister who was asked whether the
Episcopal Church was the only path to salvation.
The minister shook his head—a bit sadly, perhaps. "No, there are other paths," he said, and
then added, "but no gentleman would choose
them." Some of our attitudes toward college
education verge dangerously on the same position.

There are some people who seem to favor almost limitless expansion of college attendance. One hears the phrase "everyone has a right to go to college." It is easy to dispose of this position in its extreme form. There are some youngsters whose mental deficiency is so severe that they cannot enter the first grade. There are a number of youngsters out of every hundred whose mental limitations make it impossible for them to get as far as junior high school. There are many more who can progress through high school only if they are placed in special programs which take into account their academic limitations. These "slow learners" could not complete high school if they were required to enroll in a college-preparatory curriculum.

It is true that some who fall in this group would not be there if it were not for social and economic handicaps. But for most of them, there is no convincing evidence that social handicaps are a major factor in their academic limitations. Children with severe or moderate intellectual limitations appear not infrequently in families which are able to give them every advantage, and in which the possibilities of treatment have been exhaustively explored. Such children can be helped by intelligent attention, but the hope that any major change can be accomplished in their academic limitations is usually doomed to disappointment.

With each higher grade an increasing number of youngsters find it difficult or impossible to keep up with the work. Some drop out. Some transfer to vocational or industrial arts programs. A great many never complete high school.

Presumably, college students should only be drawn from the group which is able to get through high school. So the question becomes: "Should all high school graduates go to college?" The answer most frequently heard is that "all should go to college who are qualified for it"— but what do we mean by *qualified?* Probably less than 1 per cent of the college-age population is qualified to attend the California Institute of Technology. There are other colleges where 10, 20, 40 or 60 per cent of the college-age population is qualified to attend.

It would be possible to create institutions with standards so low that 90 per cent of the college-age population could qualify. In order to do so it would be necessary only to water down the curriculum and provide simpler subjects. Pushed to its extreme, the logic of this position would lead us to the establishment of institutions at about the intellectual level of summer camps. We could then include almost all of the population in these make-believe colleges.

Let us pursue this depressing thought. If it were certain that almost all of the eighteen- to twenty-two-year-old population could benefit greatly by full-time attendance at "colleges" of this sort, no one could reasonably object. But one must look with extreme skepticism upon the notion that all high school graduates can profit by continued formal schooling. There is no question that they can profit by continued *education*. But the character of this education will vary from one youngster to the next. Some will profit by continued book learning; others by some kind of vocational training; still others by learning on the job. Others may require other kinds of growth experiences.

Because college has gained extraordinary prestige, we are tempted to assume that the only useful learning and growth comes from attending such an institution, listening to professors talk from platforms, and reproducing required information on occasions called examinations. This is an extremely constricting notion. Even in the case of intellectually gifted individuals, it is a mistake to assume that the only kind of learning they can accomplish is in school. Many gifted individuals might be better off if they could be exposed to alternative growth experiences.

In the case of the youngster who is not very talented academically, forced continuance of education may simply prolong a situation in which he is doomed to failure. Many a youngster of low ability has been kept on pointlessly in a school which taught him no vocation, exposed him to continuous failure and then sent him out into the world with a record which convinced employers that he must forever afterward be limited to unskilled or semi-skilled work. This is not a sensible way to conserve human resources.

Properly understood, the college or university is the instrument of *one kind of further education of those whose capacities fit them for that kind of education*. It should not be regarded as the sole means of establishing one's human worth. It should not be seen as the unique key to happiness, self-respect and inner confidence.

We have all done our bit to foster these misconceptions. And the root of the difficulty is our bad habit of assuming that the only meaningful life is the "successful" life, defining success in terms of high personal attainment in the world's eyes. Today attendance at college has become virtually a prerequisite of high attainment in the world's eyes, so that it becomes, in the false value framework we have created, the only passport to a meaningful life. No wonder our colleges are crowded.

The crowding in our colleges is less regrettable than the confusion in our values. *Human dignity and worth should be assessed only in terms of those qualities of mind and spirit that are within the reach of every human being*.

This is not to say that we should not value achievement. We should value it exceedingly. It is simply to say that achievement should not be confused with human worth. Our recognition of the dignity and worth of the individual is based upon moral imperatives and should be of universal application. In other words, everyone has a "right" to that recognition. Being a college graduate involves qualities of mind which can never be universally possessed. Everyone does not have a right to be a college graduate, any more than everyone has a right to run a four-minute mile.

What we are really seeking is what James Conant had in mind when he said that the American people are concerned not only for equality of opportunity but for equality of respect. Every human being wishes to be respected regardless of his ability, and in moral terms we are bound to grant him that right. The more we allow the impression to get abroad that only the college man or woman is worthy of respect in our society, the more we contribute to a fatal confusion which works to the injury of all concerned. If we make the confusing assumption that college is the sole cradle of human dignity, need we be surprised that every citizen demands to be rocked in that cradle?

The Need for Institutional Diversity

But a scaling down of our emphasis on college education is only part of the answer. Another important part of the answer must be a greatly increased emphasis upon individual differences, upon many kinds of talent, upon the immensely varied ways in which individual potentialities may be realized.

If we develop such an indomitable concern for individual differences, we will learn to laugh at the assumption that a college education is the only avenue to human dignity and social worth.

We would educate some youngsters by sending them on to college. We would educate others in other ways. We would develop an enormous variety of patterns to fit the enormous variety of individuals. And no pattern would be regarded as socially superior or involving greater human dignity than any other pattern.

But the plain fact is that college education is firmly associated in the public mind with personal advancement, upward social mobility, market value and self-esteem. And if enough of the American people believe that one must attend college in order to be accorded respect and confidence, then the very unanimity of opinion makes the generalization true.

It is particularly true, unfortunately, in the crude categories of the employment file. A cynical friend of mine said recently, "Everyone has two personalities these days—the one under his hat and the one in his employment file. The latter is the most important—and it is made up of primitive categories. Have you held too many jobs? (Never mind why.) Did you go to a good college? (Never mind if you were the campus beachcomber.) Does your job record show a steady rise in responsibilities? (Never mind if you played politics every inch of the way.)"

If we are to do justice to individual differences, if we are to provide suitable education for each of the young men and women who crowd into our colleges and universities, then we must cultivate diversity in our higher educa-

tional system to correspond to the diversity of
the clientele. There is no other way to handle
within one system the enormously disparate human capacities, levels of preparedness and motivations which flow into our colleges and universities.

But we cannot hope to create or to maintain
such diversity unless we honor the various aspects of that diversity. Each of the different kinds
of institutions has a significant part to play in
creating the total pattern, and each should be
allowed to play its role with honor and recognition.

We do not want all institutions to be alike.
We want institutions to develop their individualities and to keep those individualities. None
must be ashamed of its distinctive features so
long as it is doing something that contributes
importantly to the total pattern, and so long as
it is striving for excellence in performance. The
highly selective, small liberal arts college should
not be afraid to remain small. The large urban
institution should not be ashamed that it is
large. The technical institute should not be
apologetic about being a technical institute.
Each institution should pride itself on the role
that it has chosen to play and on the special
contribution which it brings to the total pattern
of American higher education.

Such diversity is the only possible answer to
the fact of individual differences in ability and
aspirations. And furthermore, it is the only

means of achieving *quality* within a framework of quantity. For we must not forget the primacy of our concern for excellence. We must have diversity, but we must also expect that every institution which makes up that diversity will be striving, in its own way, for excellence. This may require a new way of thinking about excellence in higher education—a conception that would be applicable in terms of the objectives of the institution. As things now stand, the word *excellence* is all too often reserved for the dozen or two dozen institutions which stand at the very zenith of our higher education in terms of faculty distinction, selectivity of students and difficulty of curriculum. In these terms it is simply impossible to speak of a junior college, for example, as excellent. Yet sensible men can easily conceive of excellence in a junior college.

The traditionalist might say, "Of course! Let Princeton create a junior college and one would have an institution of unquestionable excellence!" That may be correct, but it may also lead us down precisely the wrong path. If Princeton Junior College were excellent, it might not be excellent in the most important way that a community college can be excellent. It might simply be a truncated version of Princeton. A comparably meaningless result would be achieved if General Motors tried to add to its line of low-priced cars by marketing the front half of a Cadillac.

We shall have to be more flexible than that in

our conception of excellence. We must develop a point of view that permits each kind of institution to achieve excellence *in terms of its own objectives*.

In higher education as in everything else there is no excellent performance without high morale. No morale, no excellence! And in a great many of our colleges and universities the most stubborn enemy of high morale has been a kind of hopelessness on the part of both administration and faculty—hopelessness about ever achieving distinction as an institution. Not only are such attitudes a corrosive influence on morale, they make it virtually certain that the institution will never achieve even that kind of excellence which is within its reach. For there *is* a kind of excellence within the reach of every institution.

In short, we reject the notion that excellence is something that can only be experienced in the most rarefied strata of higher education. It may be experienced at every level and in every serious kind of higher education. And not only may it be experienced everywhere, but we must *demand* it everywhere. We must ask for excellence in every form which higher education takes. We should not ask it lightly or amiably or good naturedly; we should demand it vigorously and insistently. We should assert that a stubborn striving for excellence is the price of admission to reputable educational circles, and that those institutions not characterized by this striving are the slatterns of higher education.

We must make the same challenging demands of students. We must never make the insolent and degrading assumption that young people unfitted for the most demanding fields of intellectual endeavor are incapable of rigorous attention to *some sort of standards*. It is an appalling error to assume—as some of our institutions seem to have assumed—that young men and women incapable of the highest standards of intellectual excellence are incapable of any standards whatsoever, and can properly be subjected to shoddy, slovenly and trashy educational fare. College should be a demanding as well as an enriching experience—demanding for the brilliant youngster at a high level of expectation and for the less brilliant at a more modest level.

It is no sin to let average as well as brilliant youngsters into college. It *is* a sin to let any substantial portion of them—average or brilliant—drift through college without effort, without growth and without a goal. That is the real scandal in many of our institutions.

Though we must make enormous concessions to individual differences in aptitude, we may properly expect that every form of education be such as to stretch the individual to the utmost of his potentialities. And we must expect each student to strive for excellence in terms of the kind of excellence that is within his reach. Here again we must recognize that there may be excellence or shoddiness in every line of human endeavor. We must learn to honor excellence (indeed to *demand* it) in every socially accepted human activity, however humble the activity, and to scorn shoddiness, however exalted the activity. As I said in another connection: "An excellent plumber is infinitely more admirable than an incompetent philosopher. The society which scorns excellence in plumbing because plumbing is a humble activity and tolerates shoddiness in philosophy because it is an exalted activity will have neither good plumbing nor good philosophy. Neither its pipes nor its theories will hold water."

Opportunities Other Than College

Not long ago the mother of two teen-age boys came to me for advice. "Roger made a fine record in high school," she explained, "and when he was a senior we had exciting discussions of all the colleges he was interested in. Now Bobby comes along with terrible grades, and when the question of his future arises a silence descends on the dinner table. It breaks my heart!"

I knew something about Bobby's scholastic limitations, which were notable, and I asked warily what I might do to help.

"The high school principal says that with his record no college will take him," she said, "and that if one did take him he wouldn't last. I can't reconcile myself to that!"

"Have you discussed any possibilities other than college?" I asked.

She shook her head. "His father says he can

get him a job driving a delivery truck. But I think he just says that to jar Bobby."

It took some time for me to explain all that I thought was deplorable in her attitude and that of her husband. Parents of academically limited children should not act as though any outcome other than college is a fate worse than death. By doing so they rule out of discussion a world of significant possibilities; and the failure to think constructively about those possibilities is a disfavor to the young person.

The great prestige which college education has achieved in our society leads us to assume—quite incorrectly—that it is the only form of continued learning after high school. The assumption is that the young person either goes to college and continues to learn, or goes to work and stops learning. Most parents, deans, counselors—indeed the young people themselves—have given little or no thought to the many ways of learning and growing which do not involve college. The result is that the path to college appears to be the only exciting possibility, the only path to self-development. No wonder many who lack the qualifications for college insist on having a try at it.

The young person who does not go on to college should look forward to just as active a period of growth and learning in the post-high school years as does the college youngster.

The nature of this continued learning will depend on the young person's interests and capacities. The bright youngster who has stayed out of college for financial reasons will require a different kind of program from that of the youngster who stayed out for lack of ability.

The majority of young people—at least, of boys—who terminate their education short of college do so because they lack academic ability. Most have had unrewarding experiences in the classroom and have a negative attitude toward anything labeled "learning" or "education." Even if they are not bitter about their school experiences, they are likely to feel that, having tried that path and failed, their salvation lies elsewhere. *What they must recognize is that there are many kinds of further learning outside formal high school and college programs. The fact that they have not succeeded in high school simply means that they must continue their learning in other kinds of situations.*

The opportunities for further education of boys and girls who leave the formal educational system are numerous and varied.

Training programs within industrial corporations have expanded enormously and constitute a respectable proportion of all education today. Apprenticeship systems are not as universal as they used to be in the skilled crafts or trades, but they are still in operation in every major industry, and offer wide opportunities for the ambitious youngster. (He must be warned, however, that in some of the older crafts and trades entry is jealously guarded; indeed in some it is held within family lines as a hereditary right.)

A few labor unions have impressive educational programs. The International Ladies Garment Workers Union, for example, conducts European tours, sponsors lecture series and offers a wide variety of courses.

Various branches of government offer jobs to high school graduates which involve an opportunity to learn while working. The Armed Services offer training in a great many occupational specialties.

Night classes in the public schools are breaking all attendance records; and more than one quarter of present attendance is in trade courses for semi-skilled or unskilled workers. These courses offer a surprising range of interesting opportunities for the young person who wishes to test his aptitudes and to develop various skills.

There also exist, in the amazingly variegated pattern of American education, many special schools—art schools, music schools, nursing schools and the like—which should be considered by the young person not going on to college. The boy who wishes to become an X-ray technician and the girl who wishes to be a practical nurse, for example, will find a great many schools throughout the country at which they may receive training.

Correspondence study offers the most flexible opportunities for study beyond high school, but the young people who do not go on to college usually have little enthusiasm for paper-and-pencil work, and that is what correspondence study amounts to. For those who can overcome this handicap, there is an open door to almost any conceivable subject. One can study accountancy or blueprint reading, creative writing or diesel mechanics, watch repairing or dressmaking, finger-printing or foreign languages, music or petroleum technology. Almost the only limits are one's own interest and ability.

Educational opportunities on radio and television continue to expand. In certain parts of the country the high school graduate can study a considerable range of subjects through this medium—e.g., salesmanship, typing, composition, reading improvement and foreign languages.

Finally, jobs themselves are a form of education. Today most young people have a wide choice of jobs. They should look at the array of jobs available not simply from the standpoint of money and convenience but from the standpoint of their own further growth. If the young man is willing to think hard about his own abilities and interests, and then to look at available jobs as opportunities for self-development, he can look forward to years of learning and growth at least as rewarding as anything a college student might experience.

The possibilities reviewed here are by no means exhaustive, but they suggest the diverse paths open to the noncollege student. Some youngsters will want to get as far away as possible from "book learning" and some will not. Some will want vocational education and others may wish to continue their general education. Some will shun anything labeled a "school" or "course." But all should somehow continue learning.

In order to help young people in this direction, the following steps are essential:

1. We must make available to young people far more information than they now have on post-high school opportunities other than college.

2. Parents, teachers and high school counselors must recognize that if the youngster who is not going to college is to continue his growth and learning he must receive as much sagacious help and counsel as a college-bound student.

3. We must do what we can to alter the negative attitude toward education held by many youngsters who fail to go on to college. They must understand that they have been exposed to only one kind of learning experience and that the failures and frustrations encountered in school are not necessarily predictive of failure in every other kind of learning.

4. We must enable the young person to understand that his stature as an individual and his value as a member of society depend upon continued learning—not just for four years or a decade, but throughout life.

chapter IX

Motivation

Who Cares?

Dan, who was twelve years old and the best ball-player in his school, was undergoing a psychological interview. The psychologist said, "What is the thing you feel you need to change to be the kind of person you'd like to be?" Dan replied, "Learn to spell. Learn to throw a knuckler that hops." [1]

If all young people were as capable as Dan of putting first things first, some of the perplexing problems facing American education would resolve themselves.

Everyone agrees that motivation is a powerful ingredient in performance. Talent without motivation is inert and of little use to the world. Lewis Terman and Catherine Cox found that historical geniuses were characterized not only by very high intelligence but by the desire to excel, by perseverance in the face of obstacles, by zeal in the exercise of their gifts. [2]

Some people may have greatness thrust upon them. Very few have excellence thrust upon them. They achieve it. They do not achieve it unwittingly, by "doin' what comes naturally"; and they don't stumble into it in the course of amusing themselves. All excellence involves discipline and tenacity of purpose.

The problem of motivation raises some questions of social strategy which are extremely perplexing—so perplexing that Americans have never been willing to face them squarely. Consider, for example, the presence in our colleges of large numbers of boys and girls who really "couldn't care less" about higher education but are there because it's the thing to do. Their presence creates problems which, if honestly faced, would be the grounds for genuine concern. We avoid that unpleasantness by the simple expedient of not facing the problems honestly. This is to be commended on grounds of comfort, but it is not the path that leads on to wisdom. Let us explore some of the issues.

Over the past thirty years, we have made it easier and easier for young people to enter our colleges and universities. We have scattered colleges so liberally that no student need go far for an education. We have lowered the financial barriers in the hope of easing the way for the qualified boy or girl who could not possibly pay for higher education. Many of our institutions have held academic requirements as low as possible in order to salvage talented young people from poor secondary schools, and in the hope that able youngsters who loafed through high school would "wake up" in college.

Now that we are entering a period of overcrowding in our colleges, the trend toward lowered barriers to higher education appears to have reversed itself—at least temporarily. But over the past three or four decades—for the country as a whole—the trend has been clear.

Important social benefits have flowed from these policies. They have brought into the colleges a considerable number of bright and ambitious youngsters who might not otherwise have continued their education.

But with every step we took along this path we also increased the flow into the system of youngsters with little or no real concern to educate themselves. If it were difficult to go to college, this type of youngster wouldn't bother. When it becomes so easy that it is simpler and pleasanter than the alternatives which present themselves, then he takes the path of least resistance. As a young Californian put it, "The college doesn't pay as well as Lockheed, but the hours are a heck of a lot better." Current efforts to salvage for higher education the tens of thousands of bright youngsters who lack the desire to go to college may bring an even larger flow of such unenterprising students into higher education.

Anyone who has ever taught could comment on the vivid differences between eager and apathetic students. A Chinese proverb says "To be fond of learning is to be at the gate of knowledge." It is almost impossible to prevent the interested student from learning. He meets the teacher more than halfway—all the way if necessary. He seeks out the situations in which he can learn. He *gets* an education in the most active sense of that term.

The apathetic student, if he is at all affected by schooling, *receives* an education. To say that teachers must meet him more than halfway understates the case: they must block all exits and trap him into learning. They must be wonderfully inventive in catching his attention and holding it. They must be endlessly solicitous in counseling him, encouraging him, awakening him and disciplining him. Every professor has observed what Lounsbury once described as "the infinite capacity of the undergraduate to resist the intrusion of knowledge."

At a Western university they tell the story of a bright and lackadaisical senior who was chided by his instructor for failing to take an interest in his studies. He responded with the following note: "I'm here because the dean tells me anyone with my IQ is a national resource. I could be making $125 a week at the electronics factory. So you and your institution are costing me about $8 for every hour in class. A hit show on Broadway costs less on an hourly rate. Are you that good?"

The flow of languid and indifferent youngsters into the colleges is not wholly indefensible. In many instances, lack of interest in education is traceable to handicaps of home background that the school and college must try to remedy. Bright youngsters with low motivation *do* represent a potential national resource, and it is important to discover whether that resource is recoverable. It is our obligation to salvage those who can be salvaged. Furthermore, there are social reasons why a society might wish to provide higher education even for those youngsters who care little about it. But we should be aware of the consequences of what we are doing. Education of the aimless and halfhearted is very arduous, very expensive and—most important—a totally different process from education of the highly motivated.

As the number of apathetic students in a college increases, there is a fundamental change in the tone of the educational process. There occurs a gradual but inevitable shift in the entire educational approach—in teaching methods, in the nature of assignments, in the curriculum and in methods of handling students. As the institution reorients itself toward educational practices suitable for youngsters of low motivation, it all too often forgets the art of dealing with youngsters of high motivation.

It applies to eager and alert youngsters the practices which it uses on less spirited individuals—assignments which do not stretch the mind, and procedures which assume a considerable degree of individual apathy. The attitude which comes to dominate a school is reflected in the forthright assertion of one progressive educator: "The school should *meet* the demands of the nature of childhood, not *make* demands." [8] In short, the classroom comes to reinforce the attitude which is cultivated by the rest of our prosperous society, namely, that the individual should never be faced with a severe challenge, that he should never be called upon for even minor sacrifices, that asking him to undertake arduous duties is a form of injustice.

One might say that this makes very little difference because eager and ambitious individuals will drive themselves to achieve, and the apathetic ones will not drive themselves in any case. In short, one might argue that our bland treatment of all young people does no harm and is at the very least humane. But the difficulty is that the degree of motivation which an individual possesses at any given time is very much affected by what is expected (or demanded) of him. Every emergency, every crisis reveals unsuspected resources of personal strength in some people and evokes heightened motivation in almost all. In speaking of the hero born of such a crisis, people say, "I didn't know he had it in him." But most of us, in fact, have a better, stouter-hearted, more vigorous self within us—a self that's deliberately a little hard of hearing but by no means stone deaf.

We all know that some organizations, some families, some athletic teams, some political groups inspire their members to great heights of personal performances. In other words, high individual performance will depend to some extent on the capacity of the society or institution to evoke it. And woe to the society that loses the gift for such evocation! When an institution, organization or nation loses its capacity to evoke high individual performance, its great days are over.

From Shirtsleeves to Shirtsleeves

The man who struggles from lowly beginnings to the top of the heap is fiercely motivated. The great difference between him and his son is that he is at the top because his spirit was indomitable and his son is at the top because he was born into the right family. There is no evidence that aspirations are inherited. And the social circumstances are apt to work negatively: not only is there no reason to expect that the son will have his father's drive; the easy conditions of his life do much to insure the opposite.

Similarly, when a group forces its way to the top—a group of pioneers, or conquerors, or immigrants, or rebels—their most precious asset is their drive, their sense of purpose, their indomitability. And that is the asset they cannot easily pass on. They can pass on their wealth and their knowledge and their influence, but they cannot pass on the memory of hardships, the will to win, the fierce determination born of struggle. They represent a selected group—a group screened for vigor and determination. In the next generation the selection process becomes inoperative. It is hardly surprising that many of the sons of the successful are less highly motivated.

The moral is that just as selection for talent produces a group with high aptitudes, so selection for high motivation produces a group with vigor, spirit and morale.

In the light of that fact, consider the implications of our way of doing things.

In our society "ease" and "easiness" have become governing principles of life, not because we consciously decided that they should, but because the whole character of our national life brings them to the fore. We have a praiseworthy desire to reduce the hardships facing anyone and everyone, and we pursue this goal through innumerable public and private channels. As parents, many of us do everything possible to reduce the difficulties facing our children. We say, "I don't want my boy to go through what I went through."

The sentiment behind all this could not be more admirable, and many of the consequences have been of benefit not just to our own people but to mankind. We are inclined to be suspicious—often rightly so—of people who question the wisdom of making life so universally easy. All too often they turn out to be ungenerous spirits who enjoy ease in their own lives but resent widespread sharing of the good things of life.

But all those who express concern for the consequences of universal ease must not be placed in that category. If they are, we shall close our ears to some very important warnings. For there *is* something to the idea that the surmounting of hardships strengthens character. There *is* something to the notion that "difficulty is the nurse of greatness." The man who speaks truthfully of the struggles of his youth and of the way they formed his character may be an extraordinarily tiresome companion—but he is not talking utter nonsense.

What are the implications of all this? The reactionary says, "It's all very simple. Stop doing things for people and let the strong man be rewarded for his strength." But this is simply another example of throwing the baby out with the bath. We shall not under any circumstances retreat from our firm intention to extend the benefits of our free society and our abundant economy to as many people as possible. We shall never retreat from our intention that every youngster be given the opportunity to realize his potentialities. We shall continue our efforts to eliminate those social conditions which create great *inequalities of hardship* among our citizens; and to combat the catastrophic and senseless misfortunes which teach men little and cost them dear. We shall continue to combat disease, poverty, ignorance, prejudice and all of the other ancient enemies of man.

But many an American who is not in the least reactionary will say, "Everything you've said about motivation convinces me of something

I've long suspected: abundance isn't good for us. We're too rich, too fat, too well supplied with everything we need."

This is probably a healthy attitude, but it is not a clearheaded view of a complex question. Abundance is not a curse and poverty is not a blessing. For every talent that poverty has stimulated it has blighted a hundred. Abundance may dull the edge of some potentially gifted people, but it makes possible the nourishing of talent on a scale which would be otherwise impossible.

What we must learn is to enjoy these benefits of abundance without getting trapped in the disadvantages. An abundant society need not be a society without challenge. The choice is ours.

I used the sons of successful men as an example of how motivation may decay from generation to generation. But many, many sons of successful men run counter to the trend. While the son may have less hardship to stimulate him, he has a model to emulate. And he often grows up in an atmosphere pervaded by high standards of performance and high expectations for his own future. Some families have succeeded in creating a tradition of high performance that has remained intact for generations.

We can, in short, create conditions which challenge and stimulate the individual. It is a healthy thing for the young person to face *some kinds* of difficulties, to have to struggle to surmount them, and to learn in the process the values of endurance, courage and strength of purpose.

We should appraise the level of motivation in our society as objectively as we appraise our public health. We might then take a more realistic attitude toward the social measures which are required to keep it at an acceptable level.

This is particularly important for the segment of the population which is to exercise leadership in the society. If one is concerned to bring into the leadership ranks of a profession or a class or a society the men best qualified to exercise that leadership, the sensible thing is to guard the door with rigorous selection procedures, rigorous procedures for testing ability, rigorous courses of preparation. And the purpose of the rigor is not simply to screen out the *less able* but to screen out the *less highly motivated*. The ones who get through will then be not only men of superior ability but men of superior character. The very fact of their surmounting difficult obstacles will have accomplished a vitally important sorting out.

We must understand that high motivation is as precious a commodity as talent and that if we do not have a system which selects for this attribute as well as for talent we shall have to resign ourselves to a good deal of flabbiness in our leadership ranks. And we must recognize that one way of bringing highly motivated people to the top is to impose barriers which must be hurdled on the way to the top.

The king in the fairytale who required that suitors for his daughter's hand pass through a series of heroic tests not only ended up with a brave, clever (and lucky) son-in-law. He ended up with a highly motivated son-in-law. Not bad state policy.

Challenge and Response

We are just beginning to understand the extent to which motivation is socially determined. Whether or not our young people are eager to learn depends very much on the kind of social environment we provide for them.

We are beginning to understand that the various kinds of talents that flower in any society are the kinds that are valued in the society. On a recent visit to Holland, my wife asked a Dutchwoman why children and adults in that country showed such an extraordinarily high incidence of language skills. "We expect it of children," the woman said simply. "We think it important."

More and more we are coming to see that high performance, particularly where children are concerned, takes place in a framework of expectation. If it is expected it will often occur. If there are no expectations, there will be little high performance.

Macaulay aserted that the reason Athenian orators were the greatest the world had ever seen was that in Athens "oratory received such encouragement as it has never since obtained."

> Genius is subject to the same laws which regulate the production of cotton and molasses. The supply adjusts itself to the demand. The quantity may be diminished by restrictions, and multiplied by bounties.[4]

Macaulay vastly oversimplifies a complex subject, but his point is sound.

The fact has implications far beyond education. It means that, as a society, we shall have only the kinds of talent we nourish, only the kinds of talent we want and expect. *Are we nourishing the kinds of talent that will create a great civilization or are we not?* In matters relating to talent and society that is not just another question. It is The Question.

One difficulty is that we shall get more or less precisely what we deserve. We cannot worship frivolity and expect our young people to scorn it. We cannot scorn the life of the mind and expect our young people to honor it. H. W. Shaw said, "To bring up a child in the way he should go, travel that way yourself once in a while." [5] Our children will respect learning if their elders respect learning. They will value the things of the mind and spirit if the society values them.

But though the child is indirectly influenced by these broader attitudes in the society as a whole, his growth depends more directly on the character of his own immediate world—his family and neighborhood. If this small world has the power to nourish and challenge his mind and spirit, the shortcomings of the larger society matter little. Thus in an earlier generation, even in the bleakest frontier community a youngster might be inspired to a lifetime of learning by parents who cared about his education.

If his immediate world *cannot* provide the stimulus and challenge he needs, then he is in trouble; and society must come to his aid. The standard means of doing this has been the school, which throughout our history has sought to reach children whose lives were culturally impoverished. Unfortunately, in some parts of the country and in some of our larger cities, the school is afflicted by the same deterioration that afflicts home and neighborhood. The best teachers—who are usually in a position to choose their own working conditions—are apt to avoid schools in the deteriorated parts of town. And public officials are apt to give better attention to schools in those parts of town in which civic leaders reside.

This connection between family or neighborhood environment and interest in education must never be forgotten in weighing the achievements of Negroes or members of other culturally disadvantaged groups. A leading educator said recently, "Any Negro who is qualified can get a college education." The statement is approximately true but dodges the big issue. The fate of most talented Negro children is sealed long, long before college. The relevant question is this: "Does the intelligent Negro child enjoy a family, neighborhood or school environment which will stimulate and nourish his gifts and inspire him to high educational effort and achievement?" For too high a proportion of Negro children the answer is clearly "No." And as long as this is true the availability of college education will be a secondary issue: most Negro children with the intellectual capacity for higher education will fall by the wayside long before they get there.

In short, early environment is vitally important. But vital as it is, we must remind ourselves that responsibility for learning and growth rests finally with the individual. We can reshape the environment to remove obstacles. We can stimulate and challenge. But in the last analysis, the individual must foster his own development. At any age, the chief resource must be the individual's own interest, drive and enthusiasm for self-fulfillment.

Even in this he may be helped. He may be helped to raise his sights and to recognize his own abilities. And he may be assisted in the development of values which will give meaning and direction to his own fulfillment. Happiness, despite popular notions to the contrary, is not best conceived as a state in which all one's wishes are satisfied and all one's hopes fulfilled. For most human beings, happiness is more surely found in striving toward meaningful goals. Education can help young people to develop such goals.

There is still another ingredient in high performance which bears mentioning. It is morale—

or confidence. Excellence is not an achievement of demoralized or hopeless individuals. I am not suggesting that those who achieve excellence are more cheerful or optimistic or carefree. They may be suffering. They may have moments of despair. They may lack self-assurance in many dimensions of their lives. But deep within them they have a hard core of conviction and self-trust that makes their achievement possible.

During World War II, one of my fellow officers in the Marine Corps made a somewhat similar point. He had spent two years training Marine recruits after he himself had returned wounded from Guadalcanal. We were talking about the discipline in Marine Corps training, and he said, "It isn't discipline that makes the difference. It's discipline plus morale. When I teach those kids what it means to be a Marine they grow eight inches taller. Without that the discipline wouldn't mean a thing. When we finish with these men, they believe in themselves."

The qualities required of a Marine and the qualities required of, let us say, a creative artist are not easily compared. But neither man can achieve excellence if demoralization strikes at the inner core of self-trust on which all great performance depends.

The Mysteries of Individual Motivation

We are a long, long way from understanding the complexities of individual motivation. We understand very imperfectly, for example, the inner pressures to excel which are present in some children and absent in others. We don't really know why, from earliest years, some individuals seem indomitable, while others are tossed about by events like the bird in a badminton game. Differences in energy and other physiological traits are partially responsible. Even more important may be the role of early experiences—relations with brothers and sisters, early successes and failures. We know, for example, that high standards may be a means of challenging and stimulating the child or, depending on the circumstances, a means of frightening and intimidating him.

Equally perplexing are the problems of motivation which emerge in adult life. These problems are not discontinuous with those of childhood—indeed, they may have the same roots—but they manifest themselves in different forms. We know a good deal about the things men work for—love, security, status, money, power and the like—and we know something about the crises of middle age brought on by early commitment to values too shallow to endure for a lifetime. But we know all too little about the remarkable differences in motivation which exist between one man and another. Why do some individuals come to defeat early and live out their lives in resignation, while others seem capable of endless renewal, rising from defeat, learning and growing, constantly discovering new resources of energy and spirit?

If we are concerned with the shortage of talent

in our society, we must inevitably give attention to those who have never really explored their talents fully, to all those who level off short of their full ceiling. If we ever learn how to salvage any respectable fraction of these, we will have unlocked a great storehouse of talent.

part four

The Ingredients of a Solution

chapter X

The Democratic Dilemma

The Paradox in Democracy

Anyone who has read this far will be keenly aware of the conflicts and tensions which surround the idea of talent in a democracy. The clash between *emphasis on individual perform-ance* and *restraints on individual performance* is observable in any society. But the conflict is nowhere more lively, more intense, and more unresolvable than in a democracy such as ours. Why? The root of the difficulty is a seeming paradox in our form of society. On the one hand, we say—more persuasively than any other form of society—"let the best man win," and we reward winners no matter what their origin. Nothing is dearer to our hearts than the notion that "anybody can be somebody," that the gifted youngster can achieve success regardless of his beginnings. But though our society surpasses others in rewarding "winners" without concern for their point of origin, it is also the form of society which gives less successful people the greatest ultimate control over the "winners." Just as the able youngster may rise from poverty to wealth, so the people may back a graduated income tax which makes him contribute much of that wealth to the common good. The man with political gifts may rise to power, but the people can write laws which limit the way he exercises that power.

This paradox creates one of the tensions which makes our society unique. There are impressive opportunities for the able individual to rise to the top. But those who do not rise are given wide latitude in writing the rules which hem him in when he gets there. When such rules are inspired by standards of fair play or by basic judgments as to what constitutes excellence, proponents of democracy can have no objection. For example, when we say "let the best man win" we must specify what we mean by "best." Most ruthless? Most brilliant? Most constructive? Most wily? This is something the whole society has a right to decide. But when the society as a whole devises rules which are calculated to inhibit excellence or stifle the person of superior gifts, then all who pray for the continued vitality of democracy must protest.

In order to see the problem in its true light, it is necessary to recognize that a society which accepts performance as the chief determinant of status—as ours does—has great charm for those whose ability, drive, aggressiveness or luck enable them to come out on top. It may have notably less charm for those who do not come out on top. The latter may be individuals of lesser ability. They may be individuals of lower motivation. They may be individuals whose excellences are not of the sort that society at this particular moment chooses to reward. Or they may simply lack a temperament that takes kindly to the knife-edge of competition. There are many individuals of great gifts in the latter group.

For whatever reason, there are large numbers of individuals who will not necessarily find unrelieved exhilaration in a system that emphasizes high performance. If these large numbers come to believe that the system exposes them unnecessarily to frustration and defeat, and if they enjoy the freedom of social action characteristic of a democracy, they will create elaborate institutional defenses to diminish the emphasis upon performance as a determinant of status. We can observe such institutional defenses not only in education but in every aspect of our national life.

Trade union practices are a veritable coral reef of accumulated defenses against extreme emphasis upon individual performance. One of the leading authorities on labor once said, "The good Lord made more slow workers than fast workers. Don't ask me why. The fast workers can look after themselves under any system. It is the business of the trade union to look after the slow ones." That is by no means the only task of the union, but the statement is correct.

The business world loves to assert its devotion to competition, but it, too, is capable of powerful defensive action if competition becomes excessive. It is just such defensive action that Brandeis was referring to when he wrote, in 1912 ". . . the right of competition must be limited in order to preserve it. For excesses of competition lead to monopoly, as excesses of liberty lead to absolutism. . . ." [1] An employee of one of the great life insurance companies once wrote to me, "I'd love to see the government agency that's more bureaucratic than we are. There's only one way to get ahead here and that is to grow old." The top corporate executive is apt to be particularly eloquent in defense of individual competition, but his ambitious subordinates will usually find that he has himself well protected against any unseemly rivalry on their part.

One can discover in any Civil Service manual innumerable rules designed to blunt the edge of excessive emphasis on performance. Rules governing seniority and tenure, although they serve other important purposes, serve this purpose also.

The academic lock step which developed in many of our schools in the 1930's and 1940's, in which all youngsters are advanced a grade per year regardless of IQ and performance, was among other things a device for preventing invidious comparisons between individuals. The underlying philosophy was vigorously stated by one educator in these terms: "Any school system in which one child may fail while another succeeds is unjust, undemocratic, and uneducational." [2]

In short, our society is full of institutional

defenses against excessive emphasis on individual performance. Among these defenses are some of the most powerful and effective restraints upon high performance ever devised.

Such defenses—in one form or another—will always be with us. In their origin they are often healthy reactions to excessive emphasis upon performance. But carried far enough these defenses too can constitute excesses and can contribute a fatal rigidity to the society.

The Rise of the Meritocracy

One way *not* to solve our problems is beautifully described in Michael Young's witty book entitled *The Rise of the Meritocracy*.[8] Young's book purports to be a description of the consequences in England between A.D. 1870 and 2033 of an ever increasing emphasis upon sheer intelligence as a criterion for social advancement. At the beginning of this period, he points out, intelligence was widely distributed among all of the social classes. There were plenty of dull people whose upper-class status was assured by birth. And there were lots of bright people in the lower strata who had never had the opportunity to exhibit their ability.

He identifies the first move towards meritocracy as the introduction of the merit system into the Civil Service in 1870. After the great wars of the twentieth century forced nations to recognize that effective use of their human resources was necessary to survival, the search for talent proceeded apace. In Young's version of history, England rejected the idea of comprehensive schools as sentimental. Talented youngsters were sorted out early and given special treatment. In one after another segment of society, the merit principle replaced other methods of determining hierarchical relationships. One of the final triumphs was when the seniority principle was abolished, so that able individuals no matter how young could move instantly to the top if their ability warranted.

> . . . when castes were abolished . . . there was still another category of people to circumvent—the class of old men. . . . [Having] the wrong man in a position of power merely because he was of a superior age was every bit as wasteful as having the wrong man in a position of power merely because his parents were of a superior class.[4]

Eventually, of course, the whole society was pretty well sifted out. All the people at the top were very, very bright, all at the bottom were very, very dull. And since the less bright people (who of course far outnumbered the others) tended to elect parliamentary representatives in their own image, the House of Commons also declined in intelligence and power. The bright people went into the Civil Service, and it became the dominant factor in government.

Finally, some elements of the ruling classes suggested that since society had sorted itself out so that all the bright people were on top, one might as well return to the old hereditary principle. It had been a bad principle, they admitted, at a time in history when many in the ruling class were stupid and many in the lower class were bright; but now, the argument ran, it would simply stabilize a healthy situation.

Despite the logic of it all, which the author sets out with great satirical skill, the system produced social tensions which resulted in uncontrollable riots.

The book is an amusing and effective sermon against a Utopia based upon rigorous and unimaginative application of the merit principle. It is not, however, a sermon which we particularly need. Our society has numerous and powerful defenses against excesses of that sort.

Where Does Wisdom Lie?

As Michael Young points out, a long-continued process of "sorting out" the population (such as we have engaged in for some years and will probably intensify) will inevitably pull a substantial portion of the gifted to the top and leave the less gifted behind. Fortunately, the sifting will never be completed. Thanks to assortative mating and the facts of genetics, both bright and dull children will continue to appear throughout society.

But despite such complications, the sifting process will go a long way in the generation immediately ahead. Barring drastic equalitarian countermoves designed to halt the search for talent, we shall move toward a society in which the most gifted and most capable people are at the top. This is what we always thought of as the ideal society. And it is the only kind of society that can hold its own in today's world.

But how will it suit the people who are not on top? Will it be any more palatable to them to be underlings in a society ruled by high IQs than in a society ruled by highborn families? Or will it be even less palatable? To the extent that the less able individual does resent the sifting out of talent, to that extent he will foster the various institutional defenses which protect him from this process—the seniority rules, the rules against "rate busting," and all the other arrangements designed to insure that high performance shall not be the chief criterion for status.

The issue is well exemplified in the problem we face with respect to gifted childen today. We are now going through a period of considerable interest in the able youngster. We went through a similar period in the 1920's. That earlier period was succeeded by an almost savage rejection of any measures designed for the gifted youngster, and insistence on precisely the same treatment for all students.

Now that enthusiasm for the gifted youngster has revived, people are willing to listen to all kinds of recommendations on this score. And some of the recommendations have been somewhat extreme.

Few of the authors of such recommendations seem to understand that if the measures designed to assist the gifted youngster are such as to arouse hostility in those who are not gifted (and their parents), there is certain to be a backlash. Children who are not gifted—and parents who do not have gifted children—are in the great majority.

Anyone who cares about excellence in education (and someone had *better* care!) must ask himself how it is possible to cultivate it in ways that do not provoke such restraining or defeating countermoves.

I believe that an answer is to be found. But it requires first that we restate the problem in somewhat more constructive terms: "How can we provide opportunities and rewards for individuals of every degree of ability so that individuals at every level will realize their full potentialities, perform at their best and harbor no resentment toward any other level?"

We have already touched upon some of the important ingredients of a solution. For example, seen in this context, our principle of multiple chances is not a sentimental compromise with efficient procedure but a measure well calculated to reduce the tensions to which our system is subject. The same may be said of the principle of avoiding labels which seem to identify some children as first-class citizens and others as second-class.

And it is in this context that one may fully understand the virtues of the American comprehensive high school. Some of our critics find it hard to see the value of this institution. They prefer the European system in which children are separated quite early (ages 10–12) into two or more quite separate educational streams. It isn't that Americans haven't thought of such an arrangement. They have even tried it here and there. But they have a positive and philosophically grounded preference for dealing with all children within the context of a single school.

Of course, within such a school it is vitally necessary to arrange for differential treatment of students at different levels of ability. This may be done in such a way as to minimize invidious distinctions between children. The best system is that advocated by James B. Conant in which students are grouped according to performance in each specific subject. A pupil might be in the top group in one subject and not in another. Thus, there is no over-all sorting out of youngsters into separate "tracks" or programs or levels. In his home room the student sits with children of every degree of ability. And all participate together in sports, dramatics, extracurricular clubs and the social life of the school. Bearing in mind the inevitable tensions which we have described—tensions which our kind of society can never escape—we can think of the comprehensive high school as an important means of creating social cohesion.

Samuel Lewis, first superintendent of common schools in Ohio, wrote in 1836:

Take fifty lads in a neighborhood, including rich and poor—send them in childhood to the same school—let them join in the same sports, read and spell in the same classes, until their different circumstances fix their business for life: some go to the field, some to the mechanic's shop, some to merchandise: one becomes eminent at the bar, another in the pulpit: some become wealthy; the majority live on with a mere competency—a few are reduced to beggary! But let the most eloquent orator, that ever mounted a western stump, attempt to prejudice the minds of one part against the other—and so far from succeeding, the poorest of the whole would consider himself insulted.[5]

In short, our society has already devised some fairly effective ways of dealing with the tensions we have been talking about. But I have yet to touch upon some of the most important missing pieces in our strategy for the management of these problems. No society will successfully resolve its internal conflicts if its only asset is cleverness in the management of these conflicts. It must also have compelling goals that are shared by the conflicting parties; and it must have a sense of movement toward these goals. All conflicting groups must have a vision that lifts their minds and spirits above the tensions of the moment. In the final chapters of the book we shall see what some of the ingredients of such a vision would be for our society.

But before turning to that final question we must have a look at problems of leadership.

chapter XI

Talent and Leadership

The Idea of a Natural Aristocracy

It has often been said that in our kind of society a "natural aristocracy" should arise to replace hereditary aristocracies—an aristocracy presumably composed of men and women whose intrinsic qualities were such as to give meaning to the term. The idea was never more vividly expressed than by Thomas Jefferson, who had the opportunity to observe old-style aristocracy at its most corrupt.

I hold it to be one of the distinguishing excellences of elective over hereditary successions, that the talents which nature has provided in sufficient proportion, should be selected by the society for the government of their affairs, rather than that this should be transmitted through the loins of knaves and fools, passing from the debauches of the table to those of the bed.[1]

But although this idea is appealing to Americans (or perhaps *because* it is appealing), it has never been subjected to hard critical examination. The time for such examination is overdue.

The writers who have talked of a natural aristocracy have differed in the meanings they have given the phrase. There would be no profit for us in an exhaustive review of these meanings, but it is necessary to look at one or two of them fairly hard.

Most academic people, if asked what the phrase ought to imply, would probably say "an aristocracy of intellect." As one academic friend of mine put it, "What other true aristocracy could there be?" But there are dissenting views which are legitimate and not anti-intellectual. Consider the words of Henry James, the elder.

There are two very bad things in this American land of ours, the worship of money and the worship of intellect. Both money and intellect are regarded as good in themselves, and you consequently see the possessor of either eager to display his possessions to the public, and win the public recognition of the fact. But intellect is as essentially *subordinate* a good as money is. It is good only as a minister and purveyor to right affections. . . .[2]

Many might disagree with James in some measure, but few would deny the grain of truth in what he says. Today we have vastly more reason to respect intellect, vastly more reason to be awed by the achievements of the human mind; but in our total scale of values it must still be a subordinate good. Our admiration for the man who puts extraordinary intellectual gifts at the service of chicanery is wry at best. We cannot admire the intellectual who lends himself to the cause of tyranny and brutality. We admire the scientist because he uses his intellectual gifts in the service of one of the highest values of our civilization—the search for truth. We would not honor him if he used the same gifts for evil purposes.

In short, intellect alone is not sufficient basis for the creation of an aristocracy. There is no certainty that an aristocracy of intellect would be more virtuous, more humane or more devoted to the dignity of the individual than the aristocracy of knaves and fools which repelled Thomas Jefferson.

Another kind of objection to an aristocracy of the intellect might be entered by the many talented individuals whose gifts do not fall strictly within the meaning of the term "intellect." They might argue that the idea of an aristocracy of intellect is on the right track but too narrowly defined—that what we need is an *aristocracy of talent*. Since it is one of the themes of this book that recognition of many varieties of excellence is a requirement for a healthy society, I would applaud this revision. I would broaden it to include all of the types of high ability which are critically important to the society.

But the criticism expressed by Henry James can be broadened too. There is nothing in the word *talent* that would lessen his concern. Indeed, he might well have quoted the comment of one of his contemporaries, H. F. Amiel:

Talent is glad enough, no doubt, to triumph in a good cause; but it easily becomes a freelance, content, whatever the cause, so long as victory follows its banner.[3]

In short, talent in itself isn't enough. As in the case of intellect, we find ourselves asking "Talent in the service of what values?" Talent in the service of truth or beauty or justice is one thing; talent in the service of greed or tyranny is quite another. In other words, neither intellect nor talent alone can be the key to a position of leadership in our society. The additional requirement is a commitment to the highest values of the society.

Talent and Responsibility

In our society it is expected that power and responsibility will go hand in hand. We cannot imagine any kind of leadership—no matter how talented—which would suit our society if it lacked this attribute. We require that those who have achieved influence in our society conduct themselves with a commitment to the values which we hold in common and a sense of their obligation to the community. We do—all too often—tolerate irresponsibility in high places, but in the long run those who wield power irresponsibly are apt to be called to account.

There is no likelihood that the American people will suspend this rule in the case of men and women of great intellectual gifts. Today many gifted individuals are enjoying a measure of influence they have never before experienced. To the extent that they do, they must demonstrate a lively devotion to the common good.

When people of talent or intellect speak of an aristocracy of talent, they usually fail to mention either responsibility or leadership.

One gets the impression that many who favor an aristocracy of talent envisage a world in which talented people simply exercise their natural gifts and by so doing receive the rewards, the adulation and the fealty which the term aristocracy connotes—with none of the annoying burdens of leadership. To most people of talent, the highest function they can perform is to use their gifts in the particular line in which they have demonstrated their virtuosity, whether it be nuclear physics or philosophy. The notion that they might have responsibilities beyond the skilled pursuit of their specialty, or that they might exercise leadership (in the active and purposeful sense of that word), is often difficult for them to accept.

But one of the functions of an aristocracy is leadership. Historically, aristocracies have occasionally taken the view that their privileged position involved no obligations of leadership. But such aristocracies did not last long.

Thomas Jefferson was quite specific in outlining his own notion of the leadership functions of the natural aristocracy. In a letter to John Adams he said:

The natural aristocracy I consider as the most precious gift of nature, for the instruction . . . and government of society. . . . May we not even say that that form of government is the best, which provides the most effectually for a pure selection of these natural *aristoi* into the offices of government? [4]

Similarly, when China, in the eighteenth and nineteenth centuries, was engaged in what was probably the most thorough effort ever made to select a governing class by examination, it was understood that the coveted membership in the gentry involved an obligation to exercise active leadership.[5]

When gifted individuals come into positions of influence and power—either through their own seeking or through the accidents of history—the society can no longer tolerate irresponsibility in them. It must expect a commitment to the larger good.

As long as their contemporaries and their own motives allow them to function apart from the world, pursuing their special lines without serious entanglement in the rest of society, their civic responsibility need be no greater than that of the average citizen. Indeed, if we are to enjoy the full benefit of certain highly creative minds, we may have to *protect* them from some kinds of responsibility. Some types of intellectual and artistic work are best done when the individual is not too much entangled with the world. We do not want every artist to participate in civic reform, nor every physicist to be an opinion leader. In a good many lines of endeavor the highest reaches of performance can only be achieved by men so absorbed in their work that they have neither time nor energy for anything else.

But if educated talent as a whole adopts this position, then it cannot also dream of an aristocracy of talent. It is possible to imagine educated talent in this country preserving its privacy and aloofness from civic responsibility. It is possible, on the other hand, to imagine it functioning as a kind of "open" aristocracy. It is not possible to imagine both.

Leadership in a Free Society

As a matter of fact, the word *aristocracy*, no matter how drastically redefined, cannot be made to fit a system of leadership as fluid and dispersed and kaleidoscopic as ours. Perhaps the reason we have thought so unclearly about the idea of a natural aristocracy is that we have never really thought clearly about leadership in a free society.

In our kind of society, leadership is perhaps as widely dispersed as in any known society. We have many kinds and levels of leadership. We have governmental leaders and industrial leaders, trade union leaders and educational leaders, leaders in commerce and leaders in the world of art, leaders in agriculture and leaders in the various professions. And in no one of these fields do the leaders recognize the superior authority of any other field.

Furthermore, in the United States leadership is exercised by all kinds of people. The leader is not a man who dresses in a distinctive fashion, sits in impressive surroundings and issues commands. He may be a politician who has convinced the people that he is fit to represent them. He may be a farmer who exercises leadership through the local farm bureau and through his capacity to command the respect of his fellow farmers. He may be a corporation executive whose business leadership and sense of responsibility have brought him a larger following. He may be a scientist who has won a commanding position in the intellectual life of the nation. He may be a labor union official who exercises leadership through the power of his union. He may be a lawyer who has gained a position in public affairs through his integrity and ability. A housewife who has taken an active role in civic matters may exercise leadership.

All of these people, taken collectively, are the country's leaders. Leadership in the United States is not a matter of scores of key individuals, nor even of hundreds, nor even of thousands—it is a matter of literally tens of thousands, even hundreds of thousands of influential men and women. These individuals, in their own organizations and communities, shape public opinion, create the climate in which public opinion is formed and determine the course of our national life.

This diversity of leadership is a product of our pluralistic way of life, and is essential to the continuance of that way of life. It gives a different cast to all questions of power and social control as these affect the United States. When Michael Young wrote about the process of selection which brought able people to the top in England, he assumed, as any Englishman would, that those at the top formed a fairly close-knit and unitary group. It would be impossible to make the same assumption in the United States. Our top people in various fields may not even know each other. Thus when we speak of able people sifting to "the top," we mean to the top of a great many fields—to the top of the labor movement as well as the press, agriculture as well as industry.

But the very fact that leadership is so widely dispersed, that it is broken down into so many fields, that it is not signalized by badges of rank —all of these things reduce the self-conscious sense of responsibility of individuals and groups who are actually exercising a powerful guiding hand in our national life. They lack a sense of their role as leaders, a sense of the obligations which they have incurred as a result of the eminence which they have achieved. They exercise the power but have no keen sense of exercising it. Or they may well recognize their leadership role with respect to their own special segment of the community but be unaware of their responsibility to the larger community. If you suggest to the influential American that he occupies a position of leadership, his most predictable response is "Who, me?"

That isn't good enough. José Marti said, "Mountains culminate in peaks, and nations in men." [6] The tens and hundreds of thousands of citizens who have achieved positions of eminence and influence in our national life must live with a powerful sense of their obligation to the community and to the nation. They are our dispersed leadership. The influential citizen—whether he is a farmer or banker or labor leader or professor or lawyer—cannot evade his responsibility to the larger community.

Furthermore, even when our leaders have been conscious of their role, they have not always been fully aware of the requirements of that role. Leaders, even in a democracy, must lead. If our citizens are to recapture the sense of mission which survival demands, then our leaders at every level must have the capacity and the vision to call it out. It is hard to expect an upsurge of devotion to the common good in response to leaders who lack the moral depth to expect or understand such devotion, or the courage to evoke it, or the stature to merit the response which follows.

In short, the varied leadership of our society must come to recognize that one of the great functions of leaders is to help a society to achieve the best that is in it.

chapter XII

The Idea of Excellence

The Many Kinds of Excellence

I have said that no society can solve its internal conflicts unless its members are lifted above the tensions of the moment by powerful shared purposes. With this in mind, let us examine certain of our own shared purposes—particularly those which bear on the problem of excellence. It will be useful to begin by reviewing our notions concerning excellence itself.

There are many varieties of excellence. This is one of those absurdly obvious truths of which we must continually remind ourselves. The Duke of Wellington, in a famous incident, revealed an enviable understanding of it. The government was considering the dispatch of an expedition to Burma to take Rangoon. The Cabinet summoned Wellington and asked him who would be the ablest general to head such an undertaking. He said, "Send Lord Combermere." The government officials protested: "But we have always understood that your Grace thought Lord Combermere a fool." The Duke's response was vigorous and to the point. "So he is a fool, and a damned fool, but he can take Rangoon." [1]

In the intellectual field alone there are many kinds of excellence. There is the kind of intellectual activity that leads to a new theory, and the kind that leads to a new machine. There is the mind that finds its most effective expression in teaching and the mind that is most at home in research. There is the mind that works best in quantitative terms, and the mind that luxuriates in poetic imagery.

And there is excellence in art, in music, in craftsmanship, in human relations, in technical work, in leadership, in parental responsibilities.

Some kinds of excellence can be fostered by the educational system, and others must be fostered outside the educational system. Some kinds —e.g., managerial—may lead to worldly success, and others—e.g., compassion—may not.

There are types of excellence that involve doing something well and types that involve being a certain kind of person. There are kinds of excellence so subjective that the world cannot even observe much less appraise them. Montaigne wrote, "It is not only for an exterior show or ostentation that our soul must play her part, but inwardly within ourselves, where no eyes shine but ours."

There is a way of measuring excellence that involves comparison between people—some are musical geniuses and some are not; and there is another that involves comparison between myself at my best and myself at my worst. It is this latter comparison which enables me to assert that I am being true to the best that is in me—or forces me to confess that I am not.

Definitions of excellence tend to be most narrow at the point where we are selecting individuals, or testing them, or training them. In the course of daily life, mature people recognize many varieties of excellence in one another. But when we are selecting, testing or training we arbitrarily narrow the range. The reasons for doing so are practical ones. Narrowing the grounds for selection is one way of making the selection process manageable. To the extent that we admit a great variety of kinds of excellence we make the task of testing virtually impossible.

Consider the relatively narrow bottleneck through which most youngsters enter a career as a scientist. What they need to a very high degree is the capacity to manipulate abstract symbols and to give the kind of intellectual response required on intelligence tests. This capacity for abstract reasoning, and for the manipulation of mathematical and verbal symbols, is useful not only on the tests but in every course they take. The capacity to understand these symbols in various combinations and to reproduce them on paper in other combinations is priceless. There are other factors which contribute to success in graduate school, but most graduate students would agree that this is the heart and soul of the matter.

On the other hand, if one looks at a group of mature scientists—in their fifties, let us say—

one finds that those who are respected have gained their reputations through exercising a remarkable variety of talents. One is honored for his extraordinary gifts as a teacher: his students are his great contribution to the world. Another is respected for the penetrating ideas he puts into the stream of the science. Another is respected—though perhaps not loved—for his devastating critical faculties. And so the list goes. Some are specialists by nature, some generalists; some creative, some plodding; some gifted in action, some in expression.

Anyone who looks at the way in which the world judges his own contemporaries will recognize the varied standards of judgment which come into play. But though in daily life we recognize a good many kinds of high performance, we rarely make this variety explicit in our thinking about excellence.

And though we admit a considerable range of excellences, we are still narrower in this respect than we should be. One way to make ourselves see this is to reflect on the diverse kinds of excellence that human beings have honored at different times and places. At any given time in a particular society, the idea of what constitutes excellence tends to be limited—but the conception changes as we move from one society to another or one century to another. Baltasar Gracián said:

It is not everyone that finds the age he deserves. . . . Some men have been worthy of a better century, for every species of good does not triumph. Things have their period; even excellences are subject to fashion.[2]

Taking the whole span of history and literature, the images of excellence are amply varied: Confucius teaching the feudal lords to govern wisely . . . Leonidas defending the pass at Thermopylae . . . Saint Francis preaching to the birds at Alviano . . . Lincoln writing the second inaugural "with malice toward none" . . . Mozart composing his first oratorio at the age of eleven . . . Galileo dropping weights from the Tower of Pisa . . . Emily Dickinson jotting her "letters to the world" on scraps of paper . . . Jesus saying, "Father, forgive them; for they know not what they do." . . . Florence Nightingale nursing the wounded at Balaclava . . . Eli Whitney pioneering the manufacture of interchangeable parts . . . Ruth saying to Naomi, "Thy people shall be my people."

The list is long and the variety is great. Taken collectively, human societies have gone a long way toward exploring the full range of human excellences. But a particular society at a given moment in history is apt to honor only a portion of the full range. And wise indeed is the society that is not afraid to face hard questions about its own practices on this point. Is it honoring the excellences which are most fruitful for its own continued vitality? To what excellences is it relatively insensitive; and what does this imply for the tone and texture of its life? Is it squandering approbation on kinds of high performance which have nothing to contribute to its creativity as a society?

If any one among us can contemplate those questions without uneasiness, he has not thought very long nor very hard about excellence in the United States.

Toning Up the Whole Society

A conception which embraces many kinds of excellence at many levels is the only one which fully accords with the richly varied potentialities of mankind; it is the only one which will permit high morale throughout the society.

Our society cannot achieve greatness unless individuals at many levels of ability accept the need for high standards of performance and strive to achieve those standards within the limits possible for them. We want the highest conceivable excellence, of course, in the activities crucial to our effectiveness and creativity as a society; but that isn't enough. If the man in the street says, "Those fellows at the top have to be good, but I'm just a slob and can act like one"— then our days of greatness are behind us. We must foster a conception of excellence which may be applied to every degree of ability and to every socially acceptable activity. A missile may blow up on its launching pad because the designer was incompetent or because the mechanic who adjusted the last valve was incompetent. The same is true of everything else in our society. We need excellent physicists and excellent mechanics. We need excellent cabinet members and excellent first-grade teachers. The tone and fiber of our society depend upon a pervasive and almost universal striving for good performance.

And we are not going to get that kind of striving, that kind of alert and proud attention to performance, unless we can instruct the whole society in a conception of excellence that leaves room for everybody who is willing to strive—a conception of excellence which means that whoever I am or whatever I am doing, provided that I am engaged in a socially acceptable activity, some kind of excellence is within my reach. As James B. Conant put it, "Each honest calling, each walk of life, has its own elite, its own aristocracy based upon excellence of performance."

We cannot meet the challenge facing our free society unless we can achieve and maintain a high level of morale and drive throughout the society. One might argue that in any society which has spread prosperity as widely as ours has, morale will be universally high. But prosperity and morale are not inseparable. It is possible to be prosperous and apathetic. It is possible to be fat and demoralized. Men must have goals which, in their eyes, merit effort and commitment; and they must believe that their efforts will win them self-respect and the respect of others.

This is the condition of society we must work toward. Then, unhampered by popular attitudes disparaging excellence, we can dedicate ourselves to the cultivation of distinction and a sense of quality. We can demand the best of our most gifted, most talented, most spirited youngsters. And we can render appropriate honor to that striving for excellence which has produced so many of mankind's greatest achievements.

It is important to bear in mind that we are now talking about an approach to excellence and a conception of excellence that will bring a whole society to the peak of performance. The gifted individual absorbed in his own problems of creativity and workmanship may wish to set himself much narrower and very much more severe standards of excellence. The critic concerned with a particular development in art, let us say, may wish to impose a far narrower and more specialized criterion of excellence. This is understandable. But we are concerned with the broader objective of toning up a whole society.

This broader objective is critically important, even for those who have set themselves far loftier (and narrower) personal standards of excellence. We cannot have islands of excellence in a sea of slovenly indifference to standards. In an era when the masses of people were mute and powerless it may have been possible for a tiny minority to maintain high standards regardless of their surroundings. But today the masses of people are neither mute nor powerless. As consumers, as voters, as the source of Public Opinion, they heavily influence levels of taste and performance. They can create a climate supremely inimical to standards of any sort.

I am not saying that we can expect every man to be excellent. It would please me if this were possible: I am not one of those who believe that a goal is somehow unworthy if everyone can achieve it. But those who achieve excellence will be few at best. All too many lack the qualities of mind or spirit which would allow them to conceive excellence as a goal, or to achieve it if they conceived it.

But many more can achieve it than now do. Many, many more can *try* to achieve it than now do. *And the society is bettered not only by those who achieve it but by those who are trying.*

The broad conception of excellence we have outlined must be built on two foundation stones —and both of them exist in our society.

1. *A pluralistic approach to values.* American society has always leaned toward such pluralism. We need only be true to our deepest inclinations to honor the many facets and depths and dimensions of human experience and to seek the many kinds of excellence of which the human spirit is capable.

2. *A universally honored philosophy of individual fulfillment.* We have such a philosophy, deeply embedded in our tradition. Whether we have given it the prominence it deserves is the question which we must now explore.

chapter XIII

The Ideal of Individual Fulfillment

The Person One Could Be

Some years ago I had a memorable conversation with the ten-year-old son of one of my fellow professors. I was walking to class and he was headed for his violin lesson. We fell into conversation, and he complained that he couldn't play any real pieces on the violin yet—only those tiresome exercises. I suggested that this would be remedied as he improved, which led him to respond with melancholy: "But I don't want to improve. I expect I may even get worse."

The idea of excellence is attractive to most people and inspiring to some. But taken alone it is a fairly abstract notion. It is not the universally powerful moving force that one might wish. We must therefore ask ourselves what are the moving and meaningful ideas that will inspire and sustain people as they strive for excellence.

In our own society one does not need to search far for an idea of great vitality and power which can and should serve the cause of excellence. It is our well-established ideal of individual fulfillment. This ideal is implicit in our convictions concerning the worth of the individual. It undergirds our belief in equality of opportunity. It is expressed in our conviction that every individual should be enabled to achieve the best that is in him.

The chief instrument we have devised to further the ideal of individual fulfillment is the educational system. But in our understandable preoccupation with perfecting that instrument, we have tended to forget the broader objectives it was designed to serve. Most Americans honor education; few understand its larger purposes. Our thinking about the aims of education has too often been shallow, constricted and lacking in reach or perspective. Our educational purposes must be seen in the broader framework of our convictions concerning the worth of the individual and the importance of individual fulfillment.

Education in the formal sense is only a part of the society's larger task of abetting the individual's intellectual, emotional and moral growth. *What we must reach for is a conception of perpetual self-discovery, perpetual reshaping to realize one's best self, to be the person one could be.*

This is a conception which far exceeds formal education in scope. It includes not only the intellect but the emotions, character and personality. It involves not only the surface, but deeper layers of thought and action. It involves adaptability, creativeness and vitality.

And it involves moral and spiritual growth. We say that we wish the individual to fulfill his potentialities, but obviously we do not wish to develop great criminals or great rascals. Learning for learning's sake isn't enough. Thieves learn cunning, and slaves learn submissiveness. We may learn things that constrict our vision and warp our judgment. We wish to foster fulfillment within the framework of rational and moral strivings which have characterized man at his best. In a world of huge organizations and vast social forces that dwarf and threaten the individual, we must range ourselves whenever possible on the side of individuality; but we cannot applaud an irresponsible, amoral or wholly self gratifying individuality.

America's greatness has been the greatness of a free people who shared certain moral commitments. Freedom without moral commitment is aimless and promptly self-destructive. It is an ironic fact that as individuals in our society have moved toward conformity in their outward behavior, they have moved away from any sense of deeply-shared purposes. We must restore *both* a vigorous sense of individuality *and* a sense of shared purposes. Either without the other leads to consequences abhorrent to us.

To win our deepest respect the individual must both find himself and lose himself. This

is not so contradictory as it sounds. We respect
the man who places himself at the service of
values which transcend his own individuality
—the values of his profession, his people, his
heritage, and above all the religious and moral
values which nourished the ideal of individual
fulfillment in the first place. But this "gift of
himself" only wins our admiration if the giver
has achieved a mature individuality and if the
act of giving does not involve an irreparable
crippling of that individuality. We cannot admire faceless, mindless servants of The State or
The Cause or The Organization who were never
mature individuals and who have sacrificed all
individuality to the Corporate Good.

Waste on a Massive Scale

In our society today, large numbers of young
people never fulfill their potentialities. Their
environment may not be such as to stimulate
such fulfillment, or it may actually be such as to
stunt growth. The family trapped in poverty
and ignorance can rarely provide the stimulus
so necessary to individual growth. The neighborhood in which delinquency and social dis-
integration are universal conditions cannot
create an atmosphere in which educational values hold a commanding place. In such surroundings, the process by which talents are blighted
begins long before kindergarten, and survives
long afterward.

The fact that large numbers of American boys

and girls fail to attain their full development must weigh heavily on our national conscience. And it is not simply a loss to the individual. At a time when the nation must make the most of its human resources, it is unthinkable that we should resign ourselves to this waste of potentialities. Recent events have taught us with sledge hammer effectiveness the lesson we should have learned from our own tradition—that our strength, creativity and further growth as a society depend upon our capacity to develop the talents and potentialities of our people.

Any adequate attack on this problem will reach far beyond formal educational institutions. It will involve not only the school but the home, the church, the playground and all other institutions which shape the individual. The child welfare society, the adoption service, the foundlings' home, the hospital and clinic—all play their part. And so do slum clearance projects and social welfare programs that seek to create the kind of family and neighborhood environment which fosters normal growth.

But it is not only in childhood that we face obstacles to individual fulfillment. Problems of another sort emerge at a later stage in the life span.

Commencement speakers are fond of saying that education is a lifelong process. And yet that is something that no young person with a grain of sense needs to be told. Why do the speakers go on saying it? It isn't that they love sentiments that are well worn with reverent handling (though they do). It isn't that they underestimate their audience. The truth is that they know something their young listeners do not know—something that can never be fully communicated. No matter how firm an intellectual grasp the young person may have on the idea that education is a lifelong process, he can never know it with the poignancy, with the deeply etched clarity, with the overtones of satisfaction and regret that an older person knows it. The young person has not yet made enough mistakes that cannot be repaired. He has not yet passed enough forks in the road that cannot be retraced.

The commencement speaker may give in to the temptation to make it sound as though the learning experiences of the older generation were all deliberate and a triumph of character—character that the younger generation somehow lacks. We can forgive him that. It is not easy to tell young people how unpurposefully we learn, how life tosses us head over heels into our most vivid learning experiences, how intensely we resist many of the increments in our own growth.

But we cannot forgive him as readily if he leaves out another part of the story. And that part of the story is that the process of learning through life is by no means continuous and by no means universal. If it were, age and wisdom would be perfectly correlated, and there would be no such thing as an old fool—a proposition sharply at odds with common experience. The sad truth is that for many of us the learning process comes to an end very early indeed. And others learn the wrong things.

The differences among people in their capacity for continued growth are so widely recognized that we need not dwell on them. They must not be confused with differences in the degree of success—as the world measures success—which individuals achieve. Many whom the world counts as unsuccessful have continued learning and growing throughout their lives; and some of our most prominent people stopped learning literally decades ago.

We still have a very imperfect understanding of why some people continue to learn and grow while others do not. Sometimes one can point to adverse circumstances as the cause of a leveling off of individual growth. But we cannot identify the conditions which have hindered or fostered development.

Of course, people are never quite as buffeted by circumstance as they appear to be. The man who experiences great personal growth as a result of some accidental circumstance may have been ready to grow in any case. Pasteur said that chance favors the prepared mind. The man defeated by circumstance might have triumphed had he been made of other stuff. We all know individuals whose growth and learning can only be explained in terms of an inner drive, a curiosity, a seeking and exploring element in their personalities. Captain Cook said, "I . . . had ambition not only to go farther than any man had even been before, but as far as it was possible for a man to go." [1] Just as Cook's restless seeking led him over the face of the earth, so other men embark on Odysseys of the mind and spirit.

It is a concern both for the individual and for the nation that moves the commencement speaker. Perhaps many men will always fall into ruts. Perhaps many will always let their talents go to waste. But the waste now exists on such a massive scale that sensible people cannot believe that it is all inevitable.

Unfortunately, the conception of individual fulfillment and lifelong learning which animates the commencement speaker finds no adequate reflection in our social institutions. For too long we have paid pious lip service to the idea and trifled with it in practice. Like those who confine their religion to Sunday and forget it the rest of the week, we have segregated the idea of individual fulfillment into one compartment of our national life, and neglect it elsewhere. We have set "education" off in a separate category from the main business of life. It is something that happens in schools and colleges. It happens to young people between the ages of six and twenty-one. It is not something—we seem to believe—that need concern the rest of us in our own lives.

This way of thinking is long overdue for a drastic change. If we believe what we profess concerning the worth of the individual, then the idea of individual fulfillment within a framework of moral purpose must become our deepest concern, our national preoccupation, our passion, our obsession. We must think of education as relevant for everyone everywhere—at all ages and in all conditions of life.

Aside from our formal educational system there is little evidence of any such preoccupation. Some religious groups are doing excellent work. Our libraries and museums are a legitimate source of pride. Adult education programs have become increasingly effective. Certain of our organizations concerned with social welfare and with mental health play profoundly important roles.

But what about moving pictures, radio and television, with their great possibilities for contributing to the growth of the individual? It would be fair to say that these possibilities have not dominated the imagination of the men who control these media. On the contrary, these media have all too often permitted the triumph of cupidity over every educational value. And what about newspapers and magazines, with their obvious potentialities for furthering the intellectual and moral growth of the individual? At best, a small fraction of the publishers accepts such a responsibility. Book publishers are less vulnerable to criticism, but they are not without fault.

Serious pursuit of the goal of individual fulfillment will carry us even farther afield. Unions, lodges, professional organizations and social clubs can all contribute importantly to individual growth and learning if they are so inclined. Only sporadically have they been so inclined. There are innumerable opportunities open to the employer who is willing to acknowledge his responsibility for furthering the individual development of men and women in his employ. Some forward-looking companies have made a highly significant beginning in accepting that responsibility.

What we are suggesting is that every institution in our society should contribute to the fulfillment of the individual. Every institution must, of course, have its own purposes and preoccupations, but over and above everything else that it does, it should be prepared to answer this question posed by society: "What is the institution doing to foster the development of the individuals within it?"

Now what does all of this mean? It means that we should very greatly enlarge our ways of thinking about education. We should be painting a vastly greater mural on a vastly more spacious wall. What we are trying to do is nothing less than to build a greater and more creative civilization. We propose that the American people accept as a universal task the fostering of individual development within a framework of rational and moral values. We propose that they accept as an all-encompassing goal the furtherance of individual growth and learning at every age, in every significant situation, in every conceivable way. By doing so we shall keep faith with our ideal of individual fulfillment and at the same time insure our continued strength and creativity as a society.

If we accept this concern for individual fulfillment as an authentic national preoccupation, the schools and colleges will then be the heart of a national endeavor. They will be committed to the furthering of a national objective and not—as they now often find themselves—swimming upstream against the interests of a public that thinks everything else more urgent. The schools and colleges will be greatly strengthened if their task is undergirded by such a powerful public conception of the goal to be sought.

And both schools and colleges will be faced with a challenge beyond anything they have yet experienced. We have said that much will depend upon the individual's attitude toward learning and toward his own growth. This defines the task of the schools and colleges. Above all they must equip the individual for a never-ending process of learning; they must gird his mind and spirit for the constant reshaping and re-examination of himself. They cannot content themselves with the time-honored process of stuffing students like sausages or even the possibly more acceptable process of training them like seals. It is the sacred obligation of the schools and colleges to instill in their students the attitudes toward growth and learning and creativity which will in turn shape the society.

With other institutions at work on other parts of this task, the schools and colleges must of course give particular attention to the intellectual aspects of growth. This is uniquely their responsibility.

If we accept without reservation these implications of our traditional belief in individual fulfillment, we shall have enshrined a highly significant purpose at the heart of our national life—a purpose that will lift all American education to a new level of meaning. We shall have accepted a commitment which promises pervasive consequences for our way of thinking about the purpose of democratic institutions. And we shall have embraced a philosophy which gives a rich personal meaning to the pursuit of excellence.

chapter XIV

The Aims of a Free People

A society that does not believe in anything will never achieve excellence. What do Americans believe in? And how ardently do they believe? It is a timely question.

We have discussed one thing that Americans do firmly believe in—the importance of the individual, and his fulfillment. As long as we are true to our deepest convictions as Americans, a concern for the individual will be a central theme in our consciousness. But concern for the individual is not enough. Free men must see their goals at two levels—the level of the individual and the level of society.

Individual fulfillment on a wide scale can occur only in a society which is designed to cherish the individual, which has the strength to protect him, the richness and diversity to stimulate and develop him, and the system of values within which he can find himself—and lose himself!—as a person. Such societies do not simply grow by themselves. They will grow—and they will survive—only if free men give devoted attention to the welfare of their society. In this sense every free man lives for himself but also lives for his society. His goal must be not only individual fulfillment but the enrichment and strengthening of his society.

Wise men see the fabric of freedom as seamless. Free societies will not survive (nor be worthy of survival) if the tradition of individual fulfillment decays from within. But it is also true that free men can survive only if free societies survive.

A free people, precisely because they prize individuality, must take special pains to insure that their shared purposes do not disintegrate. Having examined our ideal of individual fulfillment, then, we must turn to an examination of our shared aims.

It is an appropriate time in history to conduct such an examination. Our society has been challenged in the most fundamental terms. I am not referring to the tensions and rivalries that enliven the international scene from day to day. These are important, but no man who is accustomed to look beyond the day's events doubts that the challenge is more profound and far-reaching than these crises. It is more than a question of who performs the most exciting feats in outer space, or who wins today's skirmish on the diplomatic front.

I do not wish to minimize our short-run problems: if we fail to deal wisely with certain of these, there may not be any long run. But the daily crises hardly need further emphasis; they press in on us with punishing force.

The long-run challenge to the United States is nothing less than a challenge to our sense of purpose, our vitality and our creativity as a people. If we fail to meet this challenge, the stratagems of the moment will not save us.

The men who founded this nation knew that in a world largely hostile to the idea of freedom, as the world was then and is now, a free society would have to prove that it is capable of—and worthy of—survival. The requirement is unchanged today. Free societies must prove their ability to make good on their promises and to keep alive their cherished values. And more than that, they must prove their vigor, their capacity to practice the disciplined virtues, their capacity to achieve excellence.

In order to understand the dimensions of the challenge, it is useful to reflect on the position in which free men find themselves today. The free society is still the exceptional society. The ideal of a free society is still unattainable or unacceptable to most of the world's peoples. Many live under governments which have no inclination to foster freedom. Others are hemmed in by their own ignorance, or by rigid social stratification. The foes of freedom are still ready to argue that the unruliness, sloth and the savage self-indulgence of men make a free society simply impractical. The world is full of people who believe that men need masters.

It is hard for Americans to realize that the

survival of the idea for which this nation stands is not inevitable. It may survive if enough Americans care enough.

It would be easier for us to grasp this truth if we weren't so blessedly comfortable. Part of our problem is how to stay awake on a full stomach. And the fateful question remains open: Can we as a people, despite the narcotic of easy living and the endless distractions of a well-heeled society, respond with vigor and courage and dedication to the demands that history has placed upon us?

All of the signs are not encouraging. At just this moment in history when we need all of our vitality and drive and capacity for sustained effort, we are in danger of losing our bearings, in danger of surrendering to a "cult of easiness." It does not require a carping critic to detect the slackness, slovenliness and bad workmanship in our national life.

Almost two centuries ago the founders of this nation set out to show the world that free men could build a great civilization. They knew that the world was watching them and they had sublime confidence that they were going to show the world something worth watching. Today you may survey vast stretches of contemporary life without detecting any sign that Americans remember that high goal. There is little agreement as to the reasons behind this state of affairs, but almost everyone agrees that it exists. Virtually everyone agrees that we need a reaffirmation of our shared purposes and a rededication to their accomplishment.

Are Americans ready for such reaffirmation and rededication? That is a question to which one can get all kinds of answers. I believe that most Americans would welcome a new burst of moral commitment and an end to the apathy, indifference and disengagement which have crept over the nation. *The best-kept secret in America today is that people would rather work hard for something they believe in than enjoy a pampered idleness.* They would rather give up their comfort for an honored objective than bask in extravagant leisure. It is a mistake to speak of dedication as a sacrifice. Every man knows that there is exhilaration in intense effort applied toward a meaningful end. Carlyle said:

It is a calumny upon men to say that they are aroused to heroic action by ease, hope of pleasure, sugar plums of any kind, in this world or the next.[1]

Ask the physician at the height of his powers whether he would trade his life, with its 18-hour days, its midnight calls, its pressures and anxieties, for a life of idleness in tranquil surroundings. Ask the retired man whether he would trade his leisure for a job in which he could apply his full powers toward something he believed in. The religious precept that you must lose yourself to find yourself is no less true at the secular level. No one who has observed the devoted scientist in his laboratory can doubt the spiritual rewards of such work. The same is true of anyone who is working toward goals that represent the highest values of his society. As John Mason Brown put it:

> Existence is a strange bargain. Life owes us little; we owe it everything. The only true happiness comes from squandering ourselves for a purpose.[2]

Of course, we all have a certain skepticism about the expenditure of effort beyond that required by the exigencies of the system. Why should I put out more effort than I am being paid to put out? What's in it for me? These are questions born of deep habituation to the marketing of one's energies in return for the necessities of life. In the arena in which such trading must go on, the considerations are valid. But we are talking now about another kind of arena and another kind of transaction. And this transaction is not subject to the same peasant craftiness. Quite the reverse. The more one gives, the more one gets.

We fall into the error of thinking that happiness necessarily involves ease, diversion, tranquility—a state in which all of one's wishes are satisfied. For most people, happiness is not to be found in this vegetative state but in *striving toward meaningful goals*. The dedicated person has not achieved all of his goals. His life is the endless pursuit of goals, some of them unattainable. He may never have time to surround himself with luxuries. He may often be tense, worried, fatigued. He has little of the leisure one associates with the storybook conception of happiness.

But he has found a more meaningful happiness. The truth is that happiness in the sense of total gratification is not a state to which man can aspire. It is for the cows, possibly for the birds, but not for us.

We want meaning in our lives. When we raise our sights, strive for excellence, dedicate ourselves to the highest goals of our society, we are enrolling in an ancient and meaningful cause—the age-long struggle of man to realize the best that is in him. Man reaching toward the most exalted goals he can conceive, man striving impatiently and restlessly for excellence, has achieved great religious insights, created great works of art, penetrated secrets of the universe and set standards of conduct which give meaning to the phrase, "the dignity of man." Hazlitt said, "Man is the only animal that laughs and weeps; for he is the only animal that is struck with the difference between what things are and what they ought to be." [3] On the other hand, man without standards, man with his eyes on the ground, has proved over and over again, in every society, and at every period of history—including the present—that human beings can be lower than the beasts, sunk in ignorance, morally and ethically blind, living a life devoid of meaning. A concern for excellence, a devotion to standards, a respect for the human mind and spirit at its best move us toward the former condition and away from the latter condition. C. G. J. Jacobi, when asked why he worked on mathematics, said "Pour l'honneur de l'esprit humain."

In short, Americans cannot and will not find happiness in apathy, aimlessness or the pursuit of momentary pleasures. They can—and I believe will—find both meaning and happiness in dedication to the highest goals of their society.

Of course, every line of behavior has its pathology, and there is pathology of dedication. People sometimes commit themselves to vicious or criminal goals. Or their commitment to worthy goals becomes so fanatical that they destroy as much as they create. And there is the "true believer" who surrenders himself to a mass movement or to dogmatic beliefs in order to escape the responsibilities of freedom. A free society does not invite that kind of allegiance. It wants only one kind of devotion, the devotion of free, rational, responsible individuals.

We shall need such dedication. The years ahead will be fateful ones not only for free men but for all men. All of our wisdom, all of our talent and vitality, all of our steadfastness will be needed. The establishment of a durable peace, the preservation of a free society, the enrichment of the tradition on which freedom depends—these cannot be achieved by listless men.

Americans have not lost the gift for devoted action. But we have, to a considerable degree, lost the habit of asking for it or expecting it—

or even understanding it. We do not assume—as we should—that the ablest and best people in our society will exhibit dedication; on the contrary, if someone does exhibit it we are surprised and impressed. We have come to think that it is something of an imposition to expect it of our fellows.

Long continued, such incapacity to understand devoted action can have only one outcome. We shall eventually lose the capacity for it. The virtues which flower in any society are the virtues that the society nourishes. The qualities of mind and character which stamp a people are the qualities which that people honor, the qualities they celebrate, the qualities they recognize instantly and respect profoundly.

Our society not only fails to ask for or expect any depth of commitment from the individual; in a curious way it even discourages such commitment. Perhaps nothing is more effective in suppressing any spirit of endeavor on the part of the individual than the overpowering size and complexity of the joint enterprise in which we are all supposed to be participants. It is not easy for the individual to see what he can do about the nation's problems. The tasks facing the frontiersman may have been grim and often frightening, but they were also obvious. Each man knew what he must do. But what does the individual do about inflation, about international organization, about the balance of trade? There are answers, but they are not self-evident.

The individual American—busy earning a living, repapering the dining room, getting the children off to school and paying the bills—doesn't hear one clear call to action. He hears a jumble of outcries and alarms, of fanfares and dirges, of voices crying "Hurry!" and voices crying "Wait!" Meanwhile he has problems of his own.

And—particularly for young people—the sense of helplessness is intensified by the appearance of successful operation which surrounds the huge glistening machinery of our society. It hums with an intimidating smoothness. How could any individual be needed much? Surely only great organizations can cope with such a giant machine. If there is a problem, surely highly coordinated teams of experts must be studying it. If there are cracks in the world, learned specialists must be measuring them.

In short, complexity seems to be the universal condition; organization the universal requirement. What can the individual do? It is not surprising that young people shrug their shoulders and find something else to talk about.

This is disturbing when one recognizes the exhilarating effect of being needed and responding to that need—whether the need is within one's family, one's community, one's nation or mankind. To be needed is one of the richest forms of moral and spiritual nourishment; and not to be needed is one of the most severe forms of psychic deprivation. There is danger in a conviction on the part of young people that they are not needed by their own community. "The sense of uselessness," said Thomas Huxley, "is the severest shock which our system can sustain." [4] The society which allows its young men and women to fall into this attitude is not simply neglecting them; it is depriving them of a powerful spiritual tonic.

It is not wholly surprising, then, that a mood of aimlessness has settled over many young people. They are not to be blamed. Nothing captures their minds and wills. Nothing spurs them to realize the best that is in them and to give that best in the service of something larger than themselves.

But the truth is that we do need our young people, and we need them desperately. Instead of scolding young people for their lack of purposefulness, our national leaders might devote a little more imagination to telling them why they are needed. Why not tell them that we've got hold of a man-sized job and need help?

The plain fact is that never in our history have we stood in such desperate need of men and women of intelligence, imagination and courage. The challenge is there—greater than any generation has ever faced. As Whitehead said, "We must produce a great age, or see the collapse of the upward striving of our race." [5]

But how should we rise to the challenge? What is expected of us? One answer—simple but profoundly important—is this: if you believe in a free society, be worthy of a free society. Every good man strengthens society. In this day of sophisticated judgments on man and society, that is a notably unfashionable thing to say, but it is true. Men of integrity, by their very existence, rekindle the belief that as a people we can live above the level of moral squalor. We need that belief; a cynical community is a corrupt community.

More than any other form of government, democracy requires a certain optimism concerning mankind. The best argument for democracy is the existence of men who justify that optimism. It follows that one of the best ways to serve democracy is to be that kind of man.

But there are tasks of a more concrete nature facing us. If our society is to flourish, large numbers of men and women must be dedicated to the performance of their roles. Dedication is a condition of the highest reaches of performance. It is not possible to buy with money the highest levels of courage, faithfulness or inspired performance. Consider the foreign service officer. We must provide ample pay for our foreign service officers; but even within the scale of monetary rewards that a wealthy nation can afford it isn't possible to buy with money the qualities and the performance needed—the competence, judgment, willingness to endure hardships, and voluntary exile from the life that Americans love. Pay is important, but only devotion and conviction will insure the desired outcome.

The same may be said of first-grade teachers, scientists, public servants and other critically important occupational groups. No society can reach heights of greatness unless in all fields critical to its growth and creativity there is an ample supply of dedicated men and women.

Whether any particular field will have enough such men and women depends partly on morale within the field itself, and partly on how highly the society as a whole values dedication. If the society understands, expects and honors dedication, then the incidence will be high. But if it assumes that dedicated men are exceedingly rare and probably a little foolish, then the incidence will be low.

Just as there must be large numbers of people who are performing critical jobs with devotion and conviction, so there must be a widespread dedication to the goals of the society at large. But can Americans achieve enough agreement on their aims to act in concert? The answer is unequivocally yes. To be sure it is not easy to suggest a list of aims on which Americans would agree; but that is as it should be. We do not want nor expect Americans to come to full agreement on a standard list of fundamental goals. We expect individual Americans to set their own priorities, not only in their personal lives but in matters affecting the common good. The result is diversity of values, diversity of opinion, diversity of aims.

But we also have shared aims. And our hope of greatness as a nation lies in these shared aims.

Some people say that we are uncertain of our shared aims. Some say we're drifting because we've achieved everything we ever wanted. Both statements are dead wrong. To say that we are confused is one way of evading the difficult tasks before us. We are not really in doubt about the more serious of our shared aims. *We know what they are. We know that they are difficult. And we know that we have not achieved them.*

Are examples needed?

We want peace with justice. We want a world that doesn't live under the fear of the bomb, a world that acknowledges the rule of law, a world in which no nation can play bully and no nation need live in fear. How many Americans would disagree with that purpose? Is it easy? Have we achieved it? Read your morning paper.

We want freedom. We don't think man was born to have someone else's foot on his neck— or someone else's hand over his mouth. We want freedom at home and we want a world in which freedom is possible. Who would disagree with that as a national aim? Who would call it easy? Who would say we've achieved it?

We believe in the dignity and worth of the individual and it is our unshakeable purpose to protect and preserve that dignity.

We believe that every person should be enabled to achieve the best that is in him, and we are the declared enemies of all conditions, such as disease, ignorance or poverty, which stunt the individual and prevent such fulfillment.

We believe in equality before the law, equal political suffrage and—dearest of all to Americans—equality of opportunity.

These items do not exhaust the list. But they are enough to demonstrate the possibility of formulating aims on which large numbers of Americans can agree. And they suggest, too, that Americans concerned for the well-being of their society and the future of mankind have a heavy agenda. If Americans are to recapture a "sense of mission," these are some of the things that that sense of mission should be about.

A list of national purposes cannot—and should not—include all of the things that individuals within the society cherish. Our kind of society gives ample scope to aims which are essentially individual in nature—such as devotion to loved ones, and religious purposes.

Although we have been talking about the secular aims of the society, everyone recognizes that most of these aims have deep roots in our religious tradition. The religious substratum in American life runs deep, and has marked us indelibly as a people. Some of the aims we have listed were conceived and brought to flower in a religious tradition. Others, though not religious in origin, have drawn powerful nourishment from religious groups and individuals. To state the matter in general terms, there is bound to be an intimate connection between a man's attitude toward these aims and those deeper dealings with "the universal and eternal" which we call religion.

There is one more thing to be said about the aims I have listed. It is characteristic of almost every item on the list that it is so well known (if not always well understood) by Americans as to be taken for granted. Yet it is also characteristic of every item on the list that it *cannot* be taken for granted. To the extent that we have made progress on these matters, we have done so through fierce and faithful effort. Courageous men and women have spent lifetimes of effort, endurance and frustration in pursuit of these aims. Others have fought and died for them. And the same measure of devotion is required today. The fact that millions of men and women have died violent deaths defending the ideal of individual freedom does not insure the survival of that ideal if we cease paying our tithes of devotion. Unlike the great pyramids, the monuments of the spirit will not stand untended. They must be nourished in each generation by the allegiance of believing men and women. Every free man, in his work and in his family life, in his public behavior and in the secret places of his heart, should see himself as a builder and maintainer of the values of his society. Individual Americans—bus drivers and editors, grocers and senators, beauty operators and ballplayers —can contribute to the greatness and strength of a free society, or they can help it to die.

chapter XV

The Pursuit of Excellence

William James said, "Democracy is on trial, and no one knows how it will stand the ordeal. . . . What its critics now affirm is that its preferences are inveterately for the inferior. So it was in the beginning, they say, and so it will be world without end. Vulgarity enthroned and institutionalized, elbowing everything superior from the highway, this, they tell us, is our irremediable destiny. . . ." [1]

William James himself did not believe that this was our destiny. Nor do I. But the danger is real and not imagined. Democracy as we know it has proved its vitality and its durability. We may be proud of its accomplishments. But let us not deceive ourselves. The specter that William James raised still haunts us.

I once asked a highly regarded music teacher what was the secret of his extraordinary success with students. He said, "First I teach them that it is better to do it well than to do it badly. Many have never been taught the pleasure and pride in setting standards and then living up to them."

Standards! That is a word for every American to write on his bulletin board. We must face the fact that there are a good many things in our character and in our national life which are inimical to standards—laziness, complacency, the desire for a fast buck, the American fondness for short cuts, reluctance to criticize slackness, to name only a few. Every thinking American knows in his heart that we must sooner or later come to terms with these failings.

But those who try to do so soon find themselves entangled in the complex and confusing issues which we have discussed in the preceding chapters. The purpose of this book has been to map some of this swampy territory so that future attempts to deal with the problem of excellence will not get bogged down in irrelevancies.

I have tried to emphasize that anyone concerned with excellence in our society must understand and take into account the social complexities that surround the subject. Only the fainthearted and the easily confused will be daunted by these complexities. Tougher-minded Americans will see that a clear view of the complexities opens the way to constructive action.

And constructive action is desperately needed. The transformations of technology and the intricacies of modern social organization have given us a society more complex and baffling than ever before. And before us is the prospect of having to guide it through changes more ominous than any we have known. This will require the wisest possible leadership. But it will also require competence on the part of individuals at every level of our society.

The importance of competence as a condition of freedom has been widely ignored (as some newly independent nations are finding to their sorrow). An amiable fondness for the graces of a free society is not enough. Keeping a free society free—and vital and strong—is no job for the half-educated and the slovenly. Free men must be competent men. In a society of free men, competence is an elementary duty. Men and women doing competently whatever job is theirs to do tone up the whole society. And the man who does a slovenly job—whether he is a janitor or a judge, a surgeon or a technician—lowers the tone of the society. So do the chiselers of high and low degree, the sleight-of-hand artists who always know how to gain an advantage without honest work. They are the regrettable burdens of a free society.

But excellence implies more than competence. It implies a striving for the highest standards in every phase of life. We need individual excellence in all its forms—in every kind of creative endeavor, in political life, in education, in industry—in short, universally.

Those who are most deeply devoted to a democratic society must be precisely the ones who insist upon excellence, who insist that free men are capable of the highest standards of performance, who insist that a free society can be a great society in the richest sense of that phrase. The idea for which this nation stands will not survive if the highest goal free men can set themselves is an amiable mediocrity.

We are just beginning to understand that free men must set their own difficult goals and be their own hard taskmasters. Since the beginning of time, most humans have had to work hard either because physical survival demanded it or because their taskmasters required it. Now, thanks to our prosperity, we don't have to put out great effort for physical survival; and a free people has no taskmasters.

With such an unprecedented release from outward pressures, free men fall easily into the error of thinking that no effort is required of them. It is easy for them to believe that freedom and justice are inexpensive commodities, always there, like the air they breathe, and not things they have to earn, be worthy of, fight for and cherish.

Nothing could be more dangerous to the future of our society.

Free men must set their own goals. There is no one to tell them what to do; they must do it for themselves. They must be quick to apprehend the kinds of effort and performance their society needs, and they must demand that kind of effort and performance of themselves and of their fellows. They must cherish what Whitehead called "the habitual vision of greatness." If they have the wisdom and courage to demand much

of themselves—as individuals and as a society—
they may look forward to long-continued vitality.
But a free society that is passive, inert and preoccupied with its own diversions and comforts
will not last long. And freedom won't save it.

Today any reference to the weaknesses of
our society is seen in the context of our international rivalries of the moment. But long, long
before such rivalries were formed we were committed, as free men, to the arduous task of
building a great society—not just a strong one,
not just a rich one, but a great society. This is a
pact we made with ourselves.

De Tocqueville was not speaking rhetorically
when he said, ". . . there is nothing more arduous than the apprenticeship of liberty." [2] And
he might have added that the apprenticeship is
unending—the unchanging requirement of a
free society's survival is that each generation
rediscover this truth. As Chesterton put it, "The
world will never be safe for democracy—it is a
dangerous trade."

But who ever supposed that it would be easy?

Notes

I. THE DECLINE OF HEREDITARY PRIVILEGE

1. R. H. Tawney, *Religion and the Rise of Capitalism,* Penguin Books, Inc., 1947, p. 166.

2. Thomas Jefferson, letter to Roger C. Weightman, June 24, 1826. Adrienne Koch and William Penn (eds.), *The Life and Selected Writings of Thomas Jefferson,* The Modern Library, Random House, 1944, pp. 729–30.

II. EQUALITY AND COMPETITIVE PERFORMANCE

1. L. A. K. S. Clappe, *The Shirley Letters from the California Mines, 1851–1852,* Alfred A. Knopf, Inc., 1949.

2. George Mason in a speech to the Fairfax Independent Company, Alexandria, Virginia, June, 1775. Quoted by Perry Miller in *Aspects of Human Equality,* L. Bryson, C. Faust, L. Finklestein, and R. M. MacIver (eds.), Harper & Brothers, 1956, p. 248.

3. G. K. Chesterton, *George Bernard Shaw,* Lane Publishing Co., 1909, p. 215.

4. Aristotle, *Politics.*

5. Lionel Trilling, *The Liberal Imagination,* The Viking Press, 1950, p. 84.

6. Merle Curti, "Intellectuals and Other People," *American Historical Review,* Vol. LX, No. 2, January, 1955, p. 267.

7. Robert Penn Warren, *All the King's Men,* Harcourt, Brace and Company, 1946, p. 101.

8. R. Bretall (ed.), *A Kierkegaard Anthology,* Princeton University Press, 1946, p. 269.

9. *The Frontier in American History,* Henry Holt & Co., Inc., 1920, p. 266.

10. Robert C. Winthrop, "Oration at the Inauguration of the Statue of Benjamin Franklin," Boston, 1836, as quoted in Irvin G. Wyllie, *The Self-Made Man in America*, Rutgers University Press, 1954, pp. 14–15.

11. Alexis de Tocqueville, *Democracy in America* (1840), Alfred A. Knopf, Inc., 1951, Vol. I, p. 249.

12. Henri Herz, "Mes Voyages en Amerique," 1866. (In Oscar Handlin, *This Was America*, Harvard University Press, 1949, p. 187.)

13. *One Man's America*, Alfred A. Knopf, Inc., 1952.

14. Statements of witnesses before the Ashley Mines Investigation Commission, Parliamentary Papers, 1842.

15. "The Conservation of Human Talent," Walter Van Dyke Bingham Lecture, Ohio State University, April 17, 1956.

III. THE THREE-WAY CONTEST

1. I Samuel 22:2.

2. Penguin Books, Inc., 1956, p. 47.

3. "The Intellectual in the English World," *The Listener*, October 4, 1956.

IV. THE GREAT TALENT HUNT

1. "Stanford's Ideal Destiny," Founder's Day Address, 1906, *Memories and Studies*, Longmans, Green & Co., 1934.

2. *Aims of Education*, The Macmillan Company, 1929.

3. Irvin G. Wyllie, *The Self-Made Man in America*, Rutgers University Press, 1954, pp. 104–105.

4. William Peden (ed.), *Notes on the State of Virginia* (1782), University of North Carolina Press, 1955.

5. Jacques Barzun, *The House of Intellect*, Harper & Brothers, 1959, p. 142.

VI. FACTS AND FANCIES ABOUT TALENT

1. Quoted in Richard Hofstadter, *Social Darwinism in American Thought*, The Beacon Press, 1955, p. 155.

2. H. G. Wells, *The Future in America*, Harper & Brothers, 1906, pp. 142–143.

3. Catherine M. Cox et al., *The Early Mental Traits of*

Three Hundred Geniuses (Genetic Studies of Genius, Vol. II), Stanford University Press, 1926.

VII. EDUCATION AS A SORTING-OUT PROCESS

1. Roger Barker in a personal letter to the author, 1956.
2. Alfred Lord Tennyson, *Idylls of the King.*
3. Henry Becque, *Querelles Littéraires,* 1890.
4. William S. Learned, "The Quality of the Educational Process in the United States and in Europe," Bulletin No. 20, The Carnegie Foundation for the Advancement of Teaching, 1927, p. 35.

VIII. COLLEGE AND THE ALTERNATIVES

1. Douglas Bush, "Education for All Is Education for None," *New York Times Magazine,* January 9, 1955, p. 13.
2. W. H. Auden (ed.), *Selected Writings of Sydney Smith,* Farrar, Straus & Cudahy, Inc., 1956, p. xiv.

IX. MOTIVATION

1. P. S. Sears, "Problems in the Investigation of Achievement and Self-Esteem Motivation," *The Nebraska Symposium on Motivation,* University of Nebraska Press, 1957.
2. Catherine M. Cox et al., *The Early Mental Traits of Three Hundred Geniuses* (Genetic Studies of Genius, Vol. II), Stanford University Press, 1926.
3. Marietta Johnson, *Youth in a World of Men,* The John Day Co., 1929, p. 261.
4. Thomas B. Macaulay, "On the Athenian Orators" (August, 1824), *Macaulay's Complete Works,* Volume XI, *Speeches, Poems and Miscellaneous Writings,* Longmans, Green & Co., 1898, p. 340.
5. Donald Day (ed.), *Uncle Sam's Uncle Josh,* Little, Brown and Co., 1953, p. 169.

X. THE DEMOCRATIC DILEMMA

1. Quoted in Richard Hofstadter, *Social Darwinism in American Thought* (rev. ed.), The Beacon Press, 1955, p. 121.

2. Marietta Johnson, *Youth in a World of Men*, The John Day Co., 1929, p. 13.

3. *The Rise of the Meritocracy, 1870–2033*, Random House, Inc., 1959.

4. *Ibid.*, p. 62.

5. Quoted in *Public Education and the Future of America*, The Educational Policies Commission, 1955, p. 18.

XI. TALENT AND LEADERSHIP

1. Thomas Jefferson, letter to George Washington, September 9, 1792, as quoted in Henry A. Washington (ed.), *The Writings of Thomas Jefferson*, Washington, 1853–54, Vol. III, p. 466.

2. Henry James, in a letter to his niece, Catherine James, 1854, as quoted in Ralph Barton Perry, *The Thought and Character of William James*, Vol. I, Little, Brown and Co., 1936, p. 135.

3. Mrs. Humphrey Ward (trans.), *Amiel's Journal*, Macmillan & Co., 1885, pp. 245–246.

4. Thomas Jefferson, letter to John Adams, October 28, 1813. Adrienne Koch and William Penn (eds.), *The Life and Selected Writings of Thomas Jefferson*, The Modern Library, Random House, 1944, p. 633.

5. Chung-li Chang, *The Chinese Gentry*, University of Washington Press, 1955.

6. Juan de Onis (trans.), *The America of José Marti*, The Noonday Press, 1953, p. 6.

XII. THE IDEA OF EXCELLENCE

1. G. W. E. Russell, *Collections and Recollections*, Harper & Brothers, 1903.

2. Baltasar Gracián, *The Art of Wordly Wisdom*, 1647 (trans.: Joseph Jacobs), The Macmillan Company, 1892, p. 12.

XIII. THE IDEAL OF INDIVIDUAL FULFILLMENT

1. Christopher Lloyd, *The Voyages of Captain Cook*, Cresset Press, London, 1949.

XIV. THE AIMS OF A FREE PEOPLE

1. Thomas Carlyle, *On Heroes, Hero-Worship and the Heroic in History,* Oxford University Press, 1946, p. 92.

2. Clifton Fadiman and Charles Van Doren (eds.), *The American Treasury,* Harper & Brothers, 1955, p. 903.

3. William Hazlitt, *Lectures on the English Comic Writers,* M. Carey & Son, 1819.

4. "On Medical Education," from *Science and Education: Essays,* D. Appleton and Company, 1896.

5. Alfred North Whitehead, preface to Wallace B. Donham, *Business Adrift,* Whittlesly House, McGraw-Hill Book Co., Inc., 1931.

XV. THE PURSUIT OF EXCELLENCE

1. "The Social Value of the College Bred," address delivered at Radcliffe College, November 7, 1907, *Memories and Studies,* Longmans, Green & Co., 1934, p. 316.

2. Alexis de Tocqueville, *Democracy in America* (1840), Alfred A. Knopf, Inc., 1951, Vol. I, p. 249.

Index

LIBRARY
BRYAN COLLEGE
DAYTON, TN. 37321

56557

PB 161